FEMINISM

IN
100 QUOTES

METRO BOOKS
New York

An Imprint of Sterling Publishing Co., Inc.
1166 Avenue of the Americas
New York, NY 10036

ISBN 978-1-4351-6779-7

For information about custom editions, special sales, and premium
and corporate purchases, please contact Sterling Special Sales
at 800-805-5489 or specialsales@sterlingpublishing.com.

Manufactured in China

2 4 6 8 10 9 7 5 3

sterlingpublishing.com

Design by Tony Seddon

FEMINISM
IN
100 QUOTES

**SARAH
HERMAN**

METRO BOOKS
New York

INTRODUCTION

Before the word "feminism" even existed, before it was debated, defined, shunned, and reclaimed, the idea behind it was expressed through letters, literature, and in public forums. This ideal of equality—that all people should have the same political, economic, and social rights, no matter what their sex and gender—has been articulated throughout the ages in various forms. From Hortensia's rousing speech in the first century BCE, calling out the unfair taxes inflicted on women, to the cries of activists at the Women's March on Washington in 2017, denouncing the gender pay gap and regressive attitudes toward reproductive rights, feminism's fury has been hard to ignore, although many have tried to do so.

While the lack of women's rights was sharply felt by the generations of women who suffered without them, historical, social, religious, and geographical factors affected progress toward achieving them. When Isotta Nogarola debated with a man about original sin, asserting Eve's greater morality, she was confronting misogynistic attitudes that were widespread in the 15th century. When, in 1855, Caroline Norton demanded a change in divorce laws, while nevertheless emphasizing her gender's inferiority, it was at a time when many women lived like unpaid servants and only rich men had a say in politics.

This book begins with the earliest recorded rumblings of discontent, with those who tried to understand women's nature and morality—the "Woman Question." It takes in some of the first published writings from those who called for education for women, and it continues through the Ages of Enlightenment and Revolution, when Olympe de Gouges and Mary Wollstonecraft publicly demanded equal citizenship for the first time.

Feminists have fought fiercely for political emancipation. The "first wave," which gained an international profile, demanded access to the echelons of power from which women had for so long been excluded. Nineteenth- and 20th-century suffragists aligned themselves with abolitionism, temperance, and labor unions; they organized and rallied en masse; they were ridiculed, arrested, and imprisoned; and they waited. And then, as access to the ballot box became commonplace for women, a second wave of feminism emerged in the 1960s, advocating sexual and reproductive liberation, fighting discrimination, and taking radical action. A third wave followed, which reclaimed gender identity and evangelized self-determination, inclusivity, and empowerment. Today, a fourth wave is emerging.

Feminist writing and activism have long been the privileges of the educated, the wealthy, and in many parts of the world, the white. History has seldom recorded the experiences of poor women, women of color, and LGBTQ women because of racism, classism, and homophobia. Unfortunately, the memorable quotes in this book reflect that. An effort has been made to include voices from a range of countries, but the majority of words come from the cultural and political West. Suffice to say, the feminism depicted here is not definitive; the experiences are not universal.

The quotations that are included come from some of feminism's most revered and most radical voices. They appear in fiction like *Jane Eyre* and *The Handmaid's Tale*, and in revolutionary treatises like *The Subjection of Women* and *The Feminine Mystique*; and they were spoken at movement-defining public meetings. They come from those whose names resonate years after their words were spoken: Elizabeth Cady Stanton, Sojourner Truth, Emmeline Pankhurst, Simone de Beauvoir, Gloria Steinem. These voices don't always agree, but they are a testament to the adversities women have faced and the change that has been accomplished. And at times they act as shameful signposts from the past, pointing to the many hurdles that still stand in the way of feminism's widely recognized goal: equality for all.

WHY do we share
the penalty when
we did not share
the guilt?

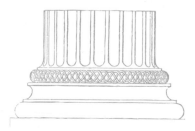

HORTENSIA

ca. 1st century BCE

SOURCE: Spoken in the Forum, Rome, and related by Appian in *Civil Wars*
DATE: ca. 42 BCE
FIELDS: Oratory/activism

During the 1st century BCE, the Roman Republic was in a state of decay, as political rivals, such as Pompey and Julius Caesar, fought for power. Civil war was rife, and this came at a great cost. While money seized from proscribed men—those declared enemies of the state, who often had bounties on their heads—helped fund these wars, more was still needed. In 42 BCE, the government imposed an extraordinarily high tax on Rome's 1,400 wealthiest women. Unable to vote or be elected, these women were furious at the suggestion that they should foot the bill. They stormed the Forum—the famous city-center plaza where processions, trials, and public speeches often occurred—and addressed the triumvirs (Rome's leaders) directly.

Hortensia was the educated daughter of Quintus Hortensius, a noted Roman orator, and as such was the natural choice to speak on behalf of the others. She argued that many of these women had already lost their fathers, husbands, and sons to proscription. "If you take away our property also," she said, "you reduce us to a condition unbecoming our birth, our manners, our sex." She addressed the unfairness of the tax, which punished women without allowing them to be involved in the political and strategic decision-making and offering them no part in "the honors, the commands, the state-craft" that they were all fighting for. It was shocking for a woman to address the crowd, but her efforts paid off. Public support meant the triumvirs changed the law, so that only 400 women would be taxed. They also decreed that men of a certain income should loan money to the war effort.

Women as well as men [...] have received from the gods the gift of

reason.

GAIUS MUSONIUS RUFUS
25–95 CE

SOURCE: As recorded in *Anthology* by Joannes Stobaeus
DATE: First century CE
FIELD: Philosophy

In ancient Rome, women were not considered equal to men under the law. A Roman woman in the 1st century CE could not hold public office, vote, or serve in the military, and she would receive at best only a basic education. She had many more rights when it came to private matters, such as managing her own financial situation, inheriting property, and getting a divorce. However, under the conservative emperor Augustus, who reigned from 27 BCE until 14 CE, there were a number of edicts that served to restrict women's behavior. For example, a widow was expected to remarry within 2 years, and a woman convicted of adultery could lose up to half her property.

Gaius Musonius Rufus was a Stoic philosopher who believed one should live for virtue rather than pleasure. He saw philosophy as something that should be studied by men and women to develop good character, with both sexes capable of understanding it. Unlike many of his contemporaries, he held the view that women should be given the same education as men, in the way that dog and horse trainers would not differentiate between the sexes of their four-legged students. He argued that courage was not something required by men only and advocated "complete companionship and concern for each other" in marriage. In contrast to the staunchly different roles of men and women in Roman society, Rufus believed that, although certain physical activities were suitable for a specific gender (outdoor work for men, spinning yarn for women), "All human work is a common responsibility [...] and nothing is necessarily prescribed for one sex or the other."

Scorn he should not render at the writer's weaker gender.

HROSWITHA OF GANDERSHEIM
ca. 935–1000 CE

SOURCE: *Basilius*
DATE: ca. late 900s CE
FIELD: Literature

Hroswitha was a 10th-century canoness, poet, and dramatist who lived and worked at Gandersheim Abbey in what is now Lower Saxony, Germany, during the days of the Ottonian dynasty. Daughters of the Saxon elite were sent to Gandersheim to receive an education, studying scripture, liberal arts, and classical literature. During her time there, Hroswitha wrote extensively, including legends, dramas, comedies, and historical works. She was acutely aware of her gender and recognized in her preface to her first book that her talent for mastering such complex verse, in spite of her "fragile female sex," was God-given. The quotation opposite is taken from the prologue to *Basilius*, a legend in which the heroine shuns a pact with the devil and helps her sinful husband to repent. It is followed by: "Who these small lines had sung with a woman's untutored tongue/But rather should he praise the Lord's celestial grace."

Hroswitha's work drew largely on the themes of martyrdom, repentance, and the strength and courage of Christian women. Her female characters' intelligence, as well as devoutness, was not in line with the Church's opinion of women, who were forbidden from approaching the altar and touching sacred vessels. Despite this, as the only dramatist in the Ottonian court at the time, and the writer of the first-known Christian plays written in Latin, Hroswitha was a pioneer, and she received support from educated patrons. Her work is believed to have influenced female poets in the 11th and 12th centuries, and after publication in 1501, interest in her writings grew.

Rape is
the greatest
possible
sorrow.

04

CHRISTINE DE PIZAN
1364–1430

SOURCE: *The Book of the City of Ladies*
DATE: 1405
FIELD: Sexual violence

Twentieth-century feminist Simone de Beauvoir once referred to Christine de Pizan as the first woman to "take up her pen in defense of her sex." Pizan was born in Venice in 1364 and was the daughter of the court astrologer for King Charles V. Later, as a widow and mother, she wrote poetry as a way of earning a living. She is best remembered, however, for her revolutionary writing about women, in which she explored their social status, criticized their portrayal in literature, and celebrated leading female figures from history.

The Book of the City of Ladies presents her in conversation with three allegorical female figures who represent the virtues of reason, rectitude, and justice. They help her to build a new city and fill it with the world's most accomplished women. As they work, they discuss a number of issues, including the importance of education for women, the idea that a woman's worth is found in her character rather than her appearance, and the horror of rape. At a time when husbands viewed their wives as property to do with as they chose, it was assumed by many that sexual violence was just a woman's lot. Rapists also justified their actions by saying that women enjoyed it. Pizan's quote opposite, while controversial, sought to present a different point of view. At the end of the book she issues a rallying cry to all women who "have loved and do love and will love virtue and morality," as she welcomes them into this new city.

But I see things—
since you move me
to reply—from
quite another and
contrary viewpoint.

05

ISOTTA NOGAROLA
1418-1466

SOURCE: *Dialogue on the Equal or Unequal Sin of Eve and Adam*
DATE: 1451
FIELD: Humanism

Considered to be the first significant female humanist, Isotta Nogarola was
part of the Italian intellectual movement that sparked the Renaissance. The
humanists believed that by studying ancient Roman and Greek texts, and the
Bible, they could put an end to the Middle Ages' cultural black hole and ignite
an educational and artistic rebirth. Many women of the elite social classes were
part of the movement, and Nogarola and her younger sister, Ginevra, were
both renowned classical scholars.

In this her most famous work, Nogarola was in dialogue with Venetian
diplomat and fellow humanist Lord Ludovico Foscarini about 5th-century
theologian Aurelius Augustine's judgment of Adam and Eve: "They sinned
unequally according to their sexes, but equally in pride." The written debate,
based on their letters to each other, caused a sensation due to its overt
discussion of gender, sin, nature, and theology, not to mention the fact it took
place between a married man and a single woman. Nogarola argued against
popular opinion that Eve deceitfully persuaded Adam to eat the forbidden fruit
and that her more fragile, less educated nature made her less culpable: "For
where there is less intellect and less constancy, there is less sin," she wrote.
This argument might raise eyebrows in contemporary feminist circles, but
it planted a seed for later feminist rethinking of the biblical story. While
Nogarola had close relationships with many famous intellectuals and political
leaders, and was widely known for her achievements, she did face opposition
to her work, causing her to stop writing for a number of years.

Woman
far excels
Man.

HEINRICH CORNELIUS AGRIPPA
1486–1535

SOURCE: *Declamation on the Preeminence and Nobility of the Female Sex*
DATE: 1529
FIELD: Humanism

In the 15th and 16th centuries, the humanist movement (see page 15) continued to debate female virtue, with some members even questioning whether women were members of the same species as men, in what became known as the "Woman Question." While a misogynist view continued to prevail, there were some men who asserted that women were in fact superior. Heinrich Cornelius Agrippa was famed for his *Declamatio*, in which he sung women's praises. The text was translated into multiple languages.

His theological arguments blamed the fall of man on Adam, who "sinned in full knowledge," and referred to the meaning of man and woman's original Hebrew names: "For Adam means earth, but Eve is translated as life. And as far as life is to be ranked above earth, so far is woman to be ranked above man." He argued that woman was made divine, from celestial matter (and one of Adam's purified ribs), making her superior by nature. He held up a woman's gift for speech, her less hairy face, and evasion of baldness as evidence of this.

Agrippa was a soldier, theologian, and occult philosopher who wrote widely about magic, but his interest in issues affecting women were apparent long before *Declamatio* was published, and he was perhaps influenced by his female patron, Archduchess Margaret of Austria. He wrote about marriage and original sin and was fiercely opposed to the witch hunts taking place in Europe during this period. In 1519 he successfully defended a woman against an accusation of witchcraft.

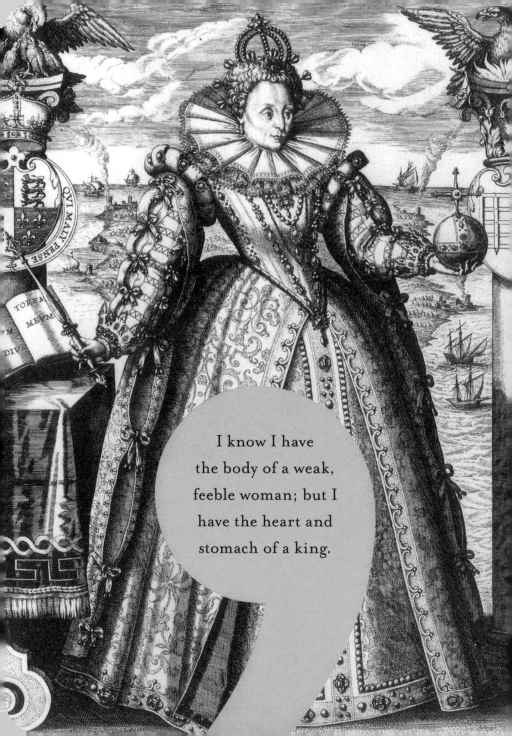

I know I have the body of a weak, feeble woman; but I have the heart and stomach of a king.

07

QUEEN ELIZABETH I
1533–1603

SOURCE: As recorded by Dr. Lionel Sharp
DATE: 1588
FIELDS: Oratory/leadership

When Queen Elizabeth I came to power in England in 1558, she also became only the second female monarch to rule the country in her own right. She reigned during a "Golden Age," remaining on the throne for 44 years and successfully overcoming many challenges from her critics. At a time when a husband had complete control over his wife, she knew that marriage and motherhood would ultimately lead to a dilution of her power. Against the advice of her counsellors to make a political alliance and produce an heir, she chose instead to rule alone, presenting herself as a "virgin" queen married only to her people.

While she was undoubtedly a strong female leader, Elizabeth is not widely thought of as a proto-feminist (that is, an early feminist thinker, before the term "feminist" entered usage). She viewed herself as exceptional, chosen by God to rule and therefore not restrained by what she saw as the limitations of the female sex. She was known to be particularly hard on the other women at court. However, the quote opposite, taken from a speech she delivered to troops at Tilbury Camp in Essex, as they waited to defend the country against Spanish invasion, can be heard as the cry of a powerful woman, loved by the people, but still having to compare herself to the men who preceded her. She saw herself as more than capable, a brave monarch who was resolved to "live and die amongst you all." Her words filled the people with pride and nationalism, and the subsequent victory against the Spanish boosted the queen's popularity even more.

If the ladies arrive less frequently to the heights of excellence than do the gentlemen, it is because of this **lack** of good education.

08

MARIE LE JARS DE GOURNAY
1565–1645

SOURCE: *Equality Between Men and Women*
DATE: 1622
FIELDS: Education/equality

French aristocrat, writer, and philosopher Marie Le Jars de Gournay was in equal parts ridiculed for her efforts to make a living as an unmarried female writer and celebrated for her scholarly works and translations. She was influential in the courts of Henry IV and Louis XIII, and was even granted a state pension in recognition of her literary prowess.

Le Jars de Gournay was not following in the footsteps of those who claimed women were, by their nature or by God's creation, superior (see page 17). Instead, she wrote in her most famous treatise, *Equality Between Men and Women*: "I am content to make women equal to men, for nature is also as opposed to superiority as to inferiority in this respect." Drawing from classical, biblical, and ecclesiastical arguments, and presenting the many historical achievements of women, she posited that prejudice alone had created the gender inequality of the day. She believed equal access to education to be key in countering misogyny, and that the lack of education was responsible for the chasm between men's and women's cultural achievements. "Women should not permit this to weaken their belief that they can achieve anything," she wrote.

Not long after her death in 1645, aged 80, her work disappeared from public discourse, despite decades of literary contributions. Toward the end of the 20th century, as feminists made a concerted effort to revive forgotten female authors, Le Jars de Gournay's writings on inequality found a new audience.

I desire to know wherefore I am

banished?

09

ANNE HUTCHINSON
1591–1643

SOURCE: From a transcript published by Puritan officials in 1637
DATE: 1637
FIELDS: Puritanism/religious persecution

While women in 17th-century Europe were pushing boundaries by challenging the lack of education available to them, in America nonconformist religious sects emerged that allowed women greater freedom of expression. In Massachusetts Bay Colony, Anne Hutchinson, the daughter of a British clergyman, held regular devotional meetings at her home in Boston. In these meetings she discussed the sermons of Puritan leader John Cotton, whom she had followed to the USA from England with her husband and children. The popularity of these religious discussions increased quickly, in part due to their nonconformist nature.

Under the governorship of John Winthrop, Puritanism in the colony grew, and tensions soon became apparent. Hutchinson's beliefs were contrary to the preaching of many Puritan ministers, who taught that a moral life was enough for God's salvation. She believed that it was only God who could offer redemption, and it could not be earned. Despite the popularity of her meetings, attended by both men and women, she was arrested for holding them. Cotton was charged alongside Hutchinson, but later cleared of committing heresy. Hutchinson, however, was banished and then excommunicated from the Church altogether. The transcript from the 1637 trial was published to garner support for the decision to banish her. Its preface emphasized her gender as part of the problem: "[A] woman has been the breeder and nourisher of all these distempers," it says. "A woman of a [...] very voluble tongue, more bold than a man, though in understanding and judgement, inferior to many women."

I am not covetous, but as ambitious as ever any of my sex was, is, or can be; which makes, that though I cannot be Henry the Fifth, or Charles the Second, yet I endeavour to be Margaret the First.

10

MARGARET CAVENDISH
1623–1673

SOURCE: *A Description of a New World Called the Blazing World*
DATE: 1666
FIELD: Science fiction

In the late 1600s, women writers and intellectuals were still rare, even among the elite classes, in large part due to their exclusion from forums for scientific and philosophical debate. In 1667, Margaret Cavendish, Duchess of Newcastle-upon-Tyne, became the first woman to attend the Royal Society in London—the world's oldest independent scientific academy—to much uproar and public debate (women were not allowed to be members until 1945). Cavendish was a Royalist who had fled England's civil war-torn shores in the 1640s for France and the court of Charles I's exiled queen, Henrietta Maria. There she met her husband, William Cavendish, who was more than happy to discuss philosophy and all the latest scientific advances. Their social circle later included the philosophers Thomas Hobbes and René Descartes.

Cavendish went on to publish numerous poems, plays, and philosophical discourses. Her vast literary output included *A Description of a New World Called the Blazing World*, in which a woman finds herself empress of a utopian realm. The book, in which she critiques scientific experimentation methods and raises questions about gender roles, is considered the first piece of science fiction to be authored by a woman. This quotation comes from the story's prefatory note, in which she addresses her audience directly as "Noble Ladies." She goes on: "And, though I have neither Power, Time nor Occasion, to be a great Conqueror, like Alexander, or Cesar; yet, rather than not be Mistress of a World, since Fortune and the Fates would give me none, I have made One of my own."

Had God intended
Women only as a finer
sort of Cattle, he would
not have made them
reasonable.

11

BATHSUA MAKIN
ca. 1600–1675

SOURCE: *An Essay to Revive the Antient Education of Gentlewomen*
DATE: 1673
FIELD: Education

Bathsua Makin, the daughter of a school teacher, was a rare thing: a 17th-century woman who had received a classical education. She used this to her advantage, becoming a tutor to Charles I's daughter, Princess Elizabeth, and then later to the Countess of Huntingdon, Lucy Hastings, and her son.

Toward the end of her life, a century before Mary Wollstonecraft published her widely read book, *A Vindication of the Rights of Women*, Makin penned an essay addressing what she saw as a moral necessity: the education of women. (It is worth noting that she categorized women as rich—"of good natural parts"—and poor—"of low natural parts"—with only the former being deemed suitable to receive an education.) She acknowledged the accomplishments of women over the ages in a range of fields but did not try to imply that women were superior or even equal to men. "They are the weaker Sex," she said, referring to her own gender, "yet capable of impressions of great things, something like to the best of Men." The essay blamed social norms and the lack of opportunity for women's perceived intellectual inferiority—a progressive position that was unusual for the time.

The essay's postscript served somewhat as an advertisement for her own recently opened school in Tottenham, London, where "by the blessing of God, Gentlewomen may be instructed in the Principles of Religion; and in all manner of Sober and Vertuous Education: More particularly, in all things ordinarily taught in other Schools."

Everything men said
about women should
be suspect, because
they are both judges
and litigants.

12

FRANÇOIS POULLAIN DE LA BARRE
1647–1725

SOURCE: *A Physical and Moral Discourse on the Equality of Both Sexes, Which Shows that It Is Important to Rid Oneself of Prejudices*
DATE: 1673
FIELDS: Philosophy/education

François Poullain de la Barre was a Parisian theology scholar, philosopher, Catholic priest, and teacher who published three feminist books between 1672 and 1675. His thinking diverged from those of his protofeminist peers, who deferred to the Bible or the ancient texts of classical thinkers to bolster their arguments. Poullain de la Barre urged his readers to rely on reason and experience, rather than preconceptions, when addressing questions of gender. He blamed existing customs and traditions for the unwavering prejudice toward women and recognized, as this quote illustrates, that men's views about women were intrinsically linked to their self-interest and should not be taken at face value.

He also raised the issue of women's lack of education. The fact that they had little access to education led to their being deemed unsuitable for certain intellectual and leadership roles in society, such as judges and professors, for example. However, because they were seen as unsuitable, and those positions were therefore not open to them, the argument was made against affording them the very education they required in order to prove themselves capable.

While his work was largely ignored in his native France, the 1677 translation of this first treatise into English was very influential. Titled *The Woman as Good as the Man*, Poullain's words and ideas were repeated numerous times over the following centuries, although his name was less well known.

MOST IN THIS DEPRAVED LATER AGE THINK A
WOMAN LEARNED AND WISE ENOUGH IF SHE CAN
DISTINGUISH HER HUSBAND'S BED FROM ANOTHER'S.

13

HANNAH WOOLLEY
1623–1675

SOURCE: *The Gentlewoman's Companion*
DATE: 1675
FIELDS: Medicine/education/domestic advice

As the author of titles such as *The Ladies Directory* and *The Cook's Guide*—offering domestic advice for women—it might be surprising to some that the quote opposite comes from Hannah Woolley. She was one of the first English women to make a living from writing, which she described as "a thing as rare for a Woman to endeavour, as obtain." Her 1675 compendium of advice included everything from "Quaint Directions for the Carving all manner of FOWL" and a recipe for "Mutton hashed the French way" to "Rules for a Gentlewomans Behaviour at a Ball," "An excellent way to dry up a Womans breast," and "A Cure for every sort of Gout." Her books served as an advertisement for her skills as a physician, despite there being many barriers preventing women from practicing medicine.

Drawing on the wisdom and knowledge Woolley garnered from her years as a governess, school mistress, and mother, she called out "Vain man," who thought women were useful only for rearing children and for keeping the house clean and tidy. "Had we the same Literature," she said, "he could find our brains as fruitful as our bodies." Like many conservative women of the era who railed against the injustices of their gender in writing, Woolley made clear she was not trying to "infuse bitter rebellion into the sweet blood of Females." She continued, with a hint of sarcasm, that she believed married women should be "loyal and loving Subjects to their lawful (though lording) Husbands."

One can perfectly well
philosophize while
cooking supper.

14

SOR JUANA INÉS DE LA CRUZ
1651-1695

SOURCE: "Response of the Poet to the Very Eminent Sor Filotea de la Cruz"
DATE: 1690
FIELDS: Religion/education

One of the only options for 17th-century Catholic women who did not wish to become a wife and mother was the life of a nun. In Mexico City, child prodigy and courtier Juana Inés de la Cruz chose to do just that. She joined the Convent of San Geronimo, so she would have "no fixed occupation that might curtail my freedom to study." And study she did, amassing a library of 4,000 books and producing plays, poems, and scholarly works. Her writing drew much attention from the Church and political leaders, in part for its controversial stance on women's rights. In one famous poem, "Foolish Men," she focuses on the irrationality of men who wanted women to fulfill their sexual desires but also remain chaste.

> *Your lover's moans give wings*
> *to women's liberty:*
> *and having made them bad,*
> *you want to find them good.*

Although her work was widely acclaimed, there were some who felt it unbefitting a nun. In 1690, she received a letter from the Bishop of Puebla, don Manuel Fernández de Santa Cruz, written under the pseudonym "Sister Filotea," in which he recommended she stop writing and focus on religious studies. "God does not want letters that give rise to presumption in woman," he wrote. The quotation opposite comes from her reply, in which she admonished men "who for the simple fact of being men think they are wise," and argued her talents were God-given and that her writing was not a choice but a necessity.

Wife and servant
are the same,
But only differ
in the name.

15

LADY MARY CHUDLEIGH
1656–1710

SOURCE: "To the Ladies"
DATE: 1703
FIELDS: Poetry/domestic servitude

From the richest ladies to the poorest, there was a common consensus that men were the masters and women their subordinates. Despite not receiving a wage from her husband, a wife, by the bonds of marriage, was considered to be the chief servant of the household (and the only one in poorer families). While some women had managerial power over their servants (or in some cases, slaves), especially in regards domestic matters, a man had power over both, not to mention over his wife's body.

Lady Mary Chudleigh was an English poet, and through her work she addressed the problems women faced in marriage, namely the obedience and deference they were expected to show to their husbands. In her poem, "To the Ladies," she drew the comparison between wives and servants, saying that married women were governed by their powerful husbands.

> *Him still must serve, him still obey,*
> *And nothing act, and nothing say,*
> *But what her haughty lord thinks fit,*
> *Who with the power, has all the wit.*

Chudleigh was a contemporary of another protofeminist, Mary Astell. Astell wrote widely about matrimony and how educating young women would lead to them making better marriage choices. In 1700, in her anonymously published *Some Reflections Upon Marriage*, she wrote that a woman had "no Reason to be fond of being a Wife, or to reckon it a Piece of Preferment when she is taken to be a Man's Upper-Servant; it is of no advantage to her in this World."

Remember the ladies and be more generous and favorable to them than your ancestors.

16

ABIGAIL ADAMS
1744–1818

SOURCE: A letter to her husband, John Adams
DATE: 1776
FIELD: Politics

In 1776, when the United States was fighting for independence from Great Britain, Abigail Adams was the wife of Congressman John Adams. With the knowledge that new laws would be passed in the wake of independence, she urged him and his fellow lawmakers to consider women more than ever. "Do not put such unlimited power into the hands of the husbands," she wrote. "If particular care and attention is not paid to the ladies, we are determined to foment a rebellion, and will not hold ourselves bound by any laws in which we have no voice or representation."

For others unable to express themselves in words, this revolutionary period saw groups of American women rising up against British rule, declaring themselves Daughters of Liberty. They were unable to fight in the war, but they boycotted non-American goods, ran businesses in their husbands' absence, and served as nurses and cooks to the army. For many it was a first taste of activism and solidarity; this would lead to their involvement in public affairs, particularly in the abolitionist movement.

In his reply, John Adams wrote: "As to your extraordinary Code of Laws, I cannot but laugh [...] your letter was the first Intimation that another Tribe more numerous and powerfull than all the rest were grown discontented." There is no evidence that Abigail Adams' words impacted the US Declaration of Independence, drawn up just a few months later; it declared, "All men are created equal." Yet when John Adams became the new country's second president, Abigail was widely considered his most trusted advisor.

WE ARE YOUR COMPANIONS

NOT YOUR SLAVES.

ETTA PALM D'AELDERS
1743–1799

SOURCE: *Discourse on the Injustice of the Laws in Favor of Men at the Expense of Women*
DATE: 1790
FIELDS: Revolution/politics

The 18th century's Age of Enlightenment brought with it an Age of Revolution, when countries transitioned from monarchical leadership to constitutional states and republics. With this came a growing demand for egalitarianism. In France, the introduction of the Declaration of the Rights of Man and of the Citizen in 1789 formed the basis of the future constitution. At the Cercle Social's Confédération des Amis de la Vérité (Friends of Truth), the first French political club to admit women, the Dutch baroness Etta Palm d'Aelders called for the movement's leaders to apply the Declaration's values to women. "Justice must be the first virtue of free men," she said, "And justice demands that the laws be the same for all beings [...] And yet everywhere, the laws favor men at the expense of women."

The short-lived National Assembly rarely discussed the emancipation of women, so the Cercle Social's revolutionary club and publishing company provided a forum for women activists to mix with prominent Parisians and politicians, and it became the birthplace of the campaign for women's rights. While suffrage was seen as important by some in this group, securing marriage and inheritance reform was viewed as a greater priority—allowing women to divorce easily and have control over their estates was seen as a requirement to helping women become true citizens. "Will you make slaves of those who have zealously contributed to making you free?" d'Aelders asked in a Cercle Social pamphlet. "No. No [...] The powers of husband and wife must be equal and separate."

Either no member of the human race has any true rights,
or else they all have the same ones.

MARIE JEAN ANTOINE NICOLAS CARITAT, MARQUIS DE CONDORCET
1743-1794

SOURCE: "On the Admission of Women to the Rights of Citizenship"
DATE: 1790
FIELDS: Suffrage/equal rights

Although fighting for change to divorce and inheritance legislation was the primary goal of France's revolutionary protofeminists, some members of the French political club Cercle Social felt strongly that women should be able to participate in the new governmental institutions alongside men. The Marquis de Condorcet was one of the first men to argue in favor of such rights, most notably when he published an essay in the *Journal de la Société de 1789*. A fierce opponent of slavery (he was the president of the Société des Amis des Noirs [Society of the Friends of Blacks]), Condorcet was known for his controversial views on pregnancy planning, gay rights, and for believing in coeducation.

"On the Admission of Women to the Rights of Citizenship" was published prior to the country's 1791 constitution, in which citizens were divided into two groups: active and passive—categories that were based largely on wealth. The majority of men were considered passive, as were all women; they were barred from the voting process and from serving as elected officials. Certain religious and racial groups were excluded from full citizenship too. Condorcet addressed this hypocrisy when he wrote: "And anyone who votes against the rights of another, whatever his religion, color, or sex, automatically forfeits his own." This radical thinker did much to shape others' views, but paid the ultimate price. When the Montagne party came to power, he was branded a traitor. In 1772 he was arrested and died in his cell shortly after.

Women, wake up; the tocsin of reason sounds throughout the universe; recognize your rights.

OLYMPE DE GOUGES
1748–1793

SOURCE: *Declaration of the Rights of Woman and Citizen*
DATE: 1791
FIELD: Equal rights

Arriving in Paris as a widow in her twenties, Marie Gouze renamed herself Olympe de Gouges and began a new life as a playwright and pamphleteer. Her dramatic works, such as *Black Slavery; or the Happy Shipwreck* and *The Philosopher Chastised, or the Supposed Cockold*, focused on controversial issues of the day: female sexual desire and abolishing slavery. Her unique voice was evident in her political pamphlets, of which she is believed to have produced around seventy. Like her contemporary, the Marquis de Condorcet, she proposed substantial reforms to the new revolutionary government, the National Assembly, including admitting women to all occupations and legalizing sexual equality.

She is best known for her 1791 publication, *Declaration of the Rights of Woman and Citizen*, a direct reply to the *Declaration of the Rights of Man and of the Citizen*— a document that was supposed to ensure universal rights. In it she rips apart the government's statement and men's acceptance of a revolution that offered them the freedoms they wanted, while still allowing them to rule over women: "Man, are you capable of being just? [...] Tell me, what gives you sovereign empire to oppress my sex." The quotation opposite comes from the end of the declaration, where she writes: "Women, when will you stop being blind? What advantages did the Revolution bring you?" After the fall of the Girondin party, with which she sided, she was arrested and condemned to death for her views. She was sent to the guillotine in 1793.

I do not wish them [women] to have power over men; but over themselves.

MARY WOLLSTONECRAFT
1759-1797

SOURCE: *A Vindication of the Rights of Woman*
DATE: 1792
FIELD: Equal rights

Hailed by many as the first feminist, Mary Wollstonecraft's *A Vindication of the Rights of Man* (1790) and *A Vindication of the Rights of Woman* (1792) addressed first the importance of the French Revolution's egalitarian ideals and then the need for sexual equality for those ideals to be fully realized. She argued that if women were offered the same education as men, they could equal men's contribution to society. Despite an unfortunate upbringing, marred by a drunken father, her mother's death, and her sister's mental-health problems, Wollstonecraft was a self-educated woman who opened a small girls' school in Stoke Newington, London. Later she would mix with other intellectuals in Paris and travel around Europe with Gilbert Imlay, the father of her first child.

Many of her views in *Rights of Woman* center on marriage and were shaped in large part by Lady Kingsborough, whom she worked for as a governess in 1786. She saw her employer's dependence on her husband, self-declared weakness, and manipulative nature as everything wrong with a woman's place in marriage. Wollstonecraft's very existence challenged the idea of matrimony—she had her first child out of wedlock—and in her 1792 work she argued that "marriage will never be held sacred till women by being brought up with men, are prepared to be their companions, rather than their mistresses." In 1797, after becoming pregnant again, she succumbed to convention and married novelist William Godwin. She died shortly after giving birth to their daughter, Mary Shelley (née Wollstonecraft Godwin), the eventual author of *Frankenstein*.

Women of England!
Women, in whatever
country ye breathe–
wherever ye breathe,
degraded–

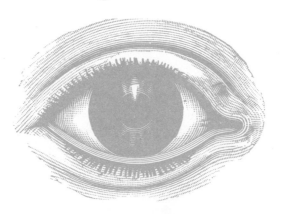

awake!

ANNA WHEELER / WILLIAM THOMPSON
1780-1848 / 1775-1833

SOURCE: *Appeal of One Half the Human Race, Women, Against the Pretensions of the Other Half, Men, to Retain Them in Political and Thence in Civil and Domestic Slavery*
DATE: 1825
FIELD: Politics

Anna Wheeler was a self-taught author and philosopher who left her alcoholic husband in Ireland to further her daughters' education and pursue her own interests in London. She was heavily influenced by Mary Wollstonecraft's (see page 45) writing and teamed up with close friend and political economist William Thompson to produce this pamphlet. It was arguably the first well-known treatise to focus on the rights of working-class and illegitimate women, rather than merely the upper classes. It called for women to be able to work alongside men, rather than remaining in the home as "domestic animals," and reminded women of men's primary reason for not wanting them in the workplace: "How fearfully would such an influx of labor and talents into the market of competition bring down their remuneration!"

While Wheeler and Thompson were critical in their writing of the men who supported and upheld inequality, they called on women to take matters into their own hands by demanding education and respect. "To obtain equal rights," they said, "the basis of equal happiness with men, you must be *respected* by them; not merely desired, like rare meats, to pamper their selfish appetites." The pamphlet's focus on mutual cooperation, in contrast to capitalism, sets it apart from other 19th-century discourses, and its authors continued to spearhead the rights of the working classes. Unfortunately, despite reaching a wide audience, the authors' voices were not loud enough to influence the Great Reform Act of 1832, which explicitly stated for the first time that women could not vote.

When both sexes

are meant to be intended,

employ not the word "man"—

but the word "person."

JEREMY BENTHAM
1748-1832

SOURCE: *Constitutional Code*
DATE: 1825
FIELDS: Social reform/philosophy

These words were transcribed from an 1825 unfinished manuscript, Jeremy Bentham's final work, titled *Constitutional Code*. In it he appears to argue for gender neutrality in pronoun usage—a very forward-thinking idea for the time. Bentham was a British social reformer and lawyer who contributed significantly to utilitarian philosophy (the idea that actions should be taken based on their usefulness and their ability to serve the largest number of people). He argued for equal educational rights, divorce rights, animal rights, and the decriminalization of homosexuality. He was a celebrated thinker in his own time, and his advice on social reform policy was sought by his contemporaries in Europe and Latin America. He was also responsible for shaping the views of his student John Stuart Mill, a future MP and advocate for women's rights.

Bentham began his defense of women's rights some 10 years before Mary Wollstonecraft's *Vindication of the Rights of Women* was published. He compared the way women around the world were virtual slaves to the patriarchal systems they lived in. Not only did he argue for the abolition of this "slavery," but he also called, in his 1817 *Plan of Parliamentary Reform*, for women to be given voting rights and the right to participate in government, and to be able to obtain a divorce more easily. However, despite his efforts, 10 years later his faith in the possibility of changing the system was waning. In *Constitutional Code* he wrote: "Why exclude the whole female sex from all participation in the constitutive power? Because the prepossession against their admission is at present too general and too intense, to afford any chance in favour of a proposal for their admission." Frankly, there was still too much opposition.

For as unseemly as it may appear now-a-days for a woman to preach, it should be remembered that nothing is impossible with God.

23

JARENA LEE
1783-1864

SOURCE: *The Life and Religious Experience of Jarena Lee*
DATE: 1836
FIELD: Religion

Almost 200 years after the trial of Anne Hutchinson in Massachusetts Bay
Colony (see page 23), women were still marginalized in much of the USA.
Yet the Protestant revival of the late 1700s, known as the Second Great
Awakening, saw women and minorities taking more prominent roles in the
new Baptist and Methodist denominations competing for followers. The
movement had a democratizing effect: To a degree, in the eyes of the faithful,
spiritual enlightenment trumped race, gender, and social status. At a time
when women's roles were changing—their home-based work was being
transferred to factories, and the Revolutionary War and western migration
had left few men to marry—they took solace in religion.

Jarena Lee was the first woman authorized to preach in the African Methodist
Episcopal (AME) Church. Born in 1783 to poor African-American parents,
Lee worked as a child servant. As an adult she joined the AME Church and,
after being turned down as a preacher, became an exhorter (delivering
personal conversion stories to the congregation). Eight years later at Bethel
Church in Philadelphia, she interrupted the male preacher, whom she felt
had "lost the spirit," to continue the sermon. Afterward, "the Bishop rose
up in the assembly," she recalled in her autobiography, and said that "he
now as much believed that I was called to that work, as any of the preachers
present." She became a traveling minister, preaching throughout the American
northeast. And "by the instrumentality of a poor coloured woman," she
wrote, "the Lord poured forth his spirit among the people."

If men and women marry those whom they do not love, they must love those whom they do not marry.

24

HARRIET MARTINEAU
1802-1876

SOURCE: *Society in America*
DATE: 1837
FIELD: Social theory

The daughter of a cloth manufacturer, Harriet Martineau was born in Norwich, England, in 1802. After her family suffered financial difficulties, she chose to support herself through her writing, rather than the alternative life of a governess. She wrote fictional short stories that shed a light on political and economic problems, and was celebrated in London circles for her intellect, despite her controversial atheist and abolitionist views.

In 1834, at the height of her fame, she traveled with a female companion to America to observe this new society. She spent nearly 2 years there, recording her findings and exploring the country's politics, economics, commerce, transport, and treatment of slaves, children, and women. The result of this was her book *Society in America*. She visited New York, Washington, Charleston, and Mississippi, among other places, and became well known. Despite her admonishments of the Americans' treatment of women, which she felt had "fallen below not only their own democratic principles, but the practice of some parts of the Old World," she praised the country's "nearly universal, more safe, more tranquil, more fortunate" approach to marriage. In the USA, divorce was easier to achieve, and women had more rights over marital property and personal wealth than their English counterparts. However, Martineau commented on the high rate of "mercenary marriages" of young women to older men, especially in the west of the country, which she believed frequently led to cases of adultery. "[Marriage] is still subject to the troubles which arise from the inequality of the parties in mind and in occupation," she said.

I long for the day when my sisters will rise, and occupy the sphere to which they are called by their high nature and destiny.

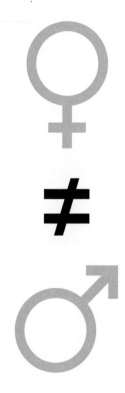

25

LUCRETIA MOTT
1793–1880

SOURCE: Sermon at Malboro Chapel, Boston
DATE: ca. 1840
FIELDS: Social reform/abolitionism

Lucretia Mott was raised a Quaker in Nantucket, Massachusetts, with the view that men and women were equally capable in the eyes of God. Her childhood confirmed that; the men often went away fishing and whaling for months at a time, while the women were left behind to make important decisions and keep the community running. The Quakers were also against slavery, declaring their position some 150 years before the Civil War. Together with her husband, James, Mott helped organize the American Anti-Slavery Society. She gave sermons, attended meetings, and even traveled to London for the World Anti-Slavery Meeting in 1840 (although Mott was not allowed to speak at the event because of her gender).

Mott found her feminist calling early on, after learning as a teenager that a male teacher was being paid more than twice that of his female counterpart. As an adult, she befriended other prominent anti-slavery and women's rights advocates, including Elizabeth Cady Stanton and Susan B. Anthony (see pages 61 and 85), with whom she would organize the first Women's Rights Convention in 1848. The quote opposite comes from her sermon titled "The Truth of God [...] The Righteousness of God." In it she wrote, "What a change would then appear in the character of woman! We should no longer find her the mere plaything of man, and a frivolous appendage of society [...] I believe that if woman would but look seriously at herself, she would learn how great an evil her nature suffers in being prevented from the exercise of her highest faculties."

There is
no wholly
masculine man,

no purely
feminine
woman.

MARGARET FULLER
1810–1850

SOURCE: *Woman in the Nineteenth Century*
DATE: 1843
FIELDS: Transcendentalism/gender

Margaret Fuller was an American journalist and transcendentalist (a 19th-century philosophical movement whose adherents believed in the inherent goodness of humanity and nature). She wrote about gender fluidity at a time when gender roles were strictly defined and largely adhered to. Her 1845 book *Woman in the Nineteenth Century* asked the reader to consider the idea that femininity and masculinity were not fixed notions, observed solely in women and men, but as "two sides of the great radical dualism" that were "perpetually passing into one another." She says that nature makes an exception to every rule, sending women warriors into battle and enabling men to care for their infants with maternal love. "Presently, she will make a female Newton and a male Syren," she writes, referring to the celebrated scientist Isaac Newton and the seductive creatures from Greek mythology.

Fuller's transcendentalist views imbued her work as a writer and feminist. The teachings of her contemporaries, such as Ralph Waldo Emerson, were in favor of a more individualistic society, with people free to express their spirituality through science, art, and nature, unbound by strict devotion to God. As a social reformer, in the years before the first Women's Rights Convention (see page 61), Fuller was keen, first and foremost, to see this individual freedom seized by women—a freedom from dependence on men, so that they could hold whichever job they wanted. "If you ask me what offices they may fill, I reply—any," she said. "I do not care what case you put; let them be sea-captains, if you will. I do not doubt there are women well fitted for such an office, and, if so, I should be as glad to see them in it."

I am no bird, and no net ensnares me:
I am a free human being with an independent will.

27

CHARLOTTE BRONTË
1816–1855

SOURCE: *Jane Eyre*
DATE: 1847
FIELD: Literature

The 19th century was an important period for English literature, and for women writers especially: from Jane Austen at the turn of the century to George Eliot (Mary Anne Evans) and Elizabeth Gaskell in the later part of it. While legal and social restrictions meant it was hard for women to embark on literary careers, many confidently wrote their own stories and published under male pseudonyms, like the Bronte sisters, Charlotte, Emily, and Anne, who wrote some of the era's most enduring works with groundbreaking female characters.

Charlotte's *Jane Eyre*, published under the name Currer Bell, is well known for the eponymous character's self-assured nature. This quotation is particularly resonant. It appears when Jane, believing her employer Rochester is engaged to be married, resolves to leave and reveals her true feelings for him, asserting her independence and naming them as equals, despite her lowlier station as a governess. "Do you think I can stay to become nothing to you?" she asks him. "Do you think I am an automaton? A machine without feelings?" Jane was an unusual heroine for the time and caused quite a stir in conservative circles. One critic, Lady Eastlake, disapproved of the novel's "illegitimate romance" and compared the book's spirit of rebellion to the uprising of the working classes, who were demanding suffrage. She commented that if the book was written by a woman, "she had long forfeited the society of her own sex."

We hold these truths to be
self-evident: that all men
and women are created
EQUAL.

28

ELIZABETH CADY STANTON
1815-1902

SOURCE: Declaration of Sentiments, Seneca Falls Convention
DATE: 1848
FIELD: Equal rights

On July 19 and 20, 1848, nearly 300 people gathered at the Wesleyan Chapel in Seneca Falls, New York, for a "convention to discuss the social, civil, and religious condition of woman." Organized by five women, including Lucretia Mott and Elizabeth Cady Stanton, the first day of the meeting saw only woman orate and debate. This lead to the drawing up of the Declaration of Sentiments, a document modeled closely on the American Declaration of Independence (which did not reference "women" in its opening remarks on equality). Stanton, who co-authored the Declaration, was a Quaker and anti-slavery activist from a wealthy family, who had been inspired to start the First Women's Rights Convention with her friend Lucretia Mott, whom she had met 8 years earlier in London.

At the radical event, which allowed men to participate on the second day, the Declaration outlined the injustices women faced in the United States, calling upon women to organize themselves and stand up for their own "unalienable rights." Twelve resolutions were passed that spoke plainly of the things women were denied, including the right to hold property, the right to divorce, and the right to a college education. Most controversially, and most importantly, it called out men for denying women the right to vote. "Having deprived her of this first right of a citizen, the elective franchise, thereby leaving her without representation in the halls of legislation, he has oppressed her on all sides." The Declaration was signed by sixty-eight women and thirty-two men, and the event led to the creation of the National Women's Rights Convention 2 years later.

Women will see
themselves forgotten,
if they do not think
about themselves.

29

LOUISE OTTO-PETERS
1819-1895

SOURCE: "Speech of a German Girl"
DATE: 1848
FIELDS: Journalism/activism

In 1848 revolutions broke out across Europe. This period of political upheaval, in which monarchies were overthrown and republics born, affected more than fifty countries. It saw smaller uprisings throughout the thirty-nine German-speaking states, during what turned out to be a failed attempt to unify the region. The wind of change gave feminists like Louise Otto-Peters the opportunity to push for women's rights, specifically, in her case, the rights of working-class women, though she herself was from a middle-class background. This quote comes from a letter she wrote, published in the *Leipzig Workers Newspaper*, to a government organization that had been created to look into the problems plaguing workers.

A year later, angered by the omission of women's rights in the formation of the Frankfurt Parliament, and with male editors refusing to publish her articles, she established her own forum, a weekly publication called *Frauen-Zeitung* (*Women's Newspaper*). Here she repeated the call: "Amid the great upheavals in which we all find ourselves, women will see themselves forgotten, if they do not think about themselves!" Her newspaper's motto was: "I enlist women citizens in the realm of freedom." She continued to follow her own advice, thinking and writing about women's rights throughout her life. In 1865, with other suffragists, she founded the General German Women's Association. Its task was "to work, with united strength, for the higher education of the female sex and for the liberation of female work from all the obstacles that stand in the way of its full development."

If it is important to teach a young boy what freedom is, it is perhaps even more important to teach a girl.

30

EUGENIE NIBOYET
ca. 1796–1883

SOURCE: La Voix des Femmes
DATE: 1848
FIELDS: Journalism/letters/education

In France, the 1848 proclamation of the Republic brought with it a much more prominent and public debate about women's rights. Suddenly, influential democratic socialists were in power, and with press restrictions lifted, feminists rallied and renewed their propaganda with a number of new publications.

Eugénie Niboyet was a prominent member of the feminist movement in France between 1830 and her death in 1882. The self-professed "woman of letters" focused her efforts on education, but also spoke out on many other issues affecting women. Feminists like her wanted state schools for girls that offered the same educational opportunities as for boys, rather than limited access to private education or tutelage from Catholic nuns. As early as 1833 in *Le conseiller des femmes*, a newspaper later edited by Niboyet, she urged other women to champion her cause. In 1848, she founded, and was president of, the *Société de la Voix des Femmes*, a women's club that promoted equality and demanded new legislation to give women electoral rights. As well as starting the first feminist daily newspaper, Niboyet did what the state would not by offering a series of courses for women in a range of subjects.

The club proved too much for some men, who publicly attacked its founder and ridiculed its ideas. "Club women, great God!" a male journalist protested. "Our mothers, our virgins, our sisters! It is absurd, it is monstrous, it is unheard of." The government banned women's clubs later that year, repressing the leading voices of the movement. It would be 20 years before French feminists would regroup.

31

SOJOURNER TRUTH
ca. 1797–1883

SOURCE: At the Women's Rights Convention, Akron, Ohio, as reported by
Frances Dana Gage in *The New York Independent* (1863)
DATE: 1851
FIELD: Equal rights

In the June 21, 1851, edition of *The Anti-Slavery Bugle*, journalist Marius
Robinson reported on the Women's Rights Convention that had taken
place two weeks before in Ohio. "One of the most unique and interesting
speeches," he wrote, "was made by Sojourner Truth, an emancipated slave.
It is impossible to transfer it to paper, or to convey any adequate idea of the
effect it produced upon the audience."

Truth was a former slave from New York who became a preacher and
committed abolitionist. In fact, many white women were concerned her speech
at the convention would focus solely on slavery, but instead, she used the
darkest experiences of her life to deliver what has become one of the most
famous women's rights orations in American history. On the second day of the
convention, male ministers had protested the women's demands for suffrage,
arguing that women were weak. Robinson recalled Truth standing up and
saying: "I have as much muscle as any man, and can do as much work as any
man. I have plowed and reaped and husked and chopped and mowed, and
can any man do more than that?"

The famous words "And ain't I a woman?" were included in Frances Dana
Gage's retelling, recorded 12 years later. Gage, an active Ohio feminist, was
the convention's president and was present when Truth delivered the speech.
In this version, the rhetorical question was repeated multiple times to great
effect. "I could work as much and eat as much as a man—when I could get it—
and bear the lash as well!" Truth exclaimed. "And ain't I a woman?"

I beseech you, pity those
mothers that are constantly
made childless by the
American slave-trade!

32

HARRIET BEECHER STOWE
1811–1896

SOURCE: *Uncle Tom's Cabin*
DATE: 1852
FIELDS: Literature/slavery/motherhood

The best-selling novel of the 19th century was *Uncle Tom's Cabin* by Harriet
Beecher Stowe. Advertised as "The greatest book of its kind," it sold over
300,000 copies in the USA in its first year alone. Its American author was
disgusted by the passage of the Fugitive Slave Act of 1850, which required
runaway slaves to be returned to their masters and made it illegal for anti-
slavery citizens in the North to harbor or help escaped slaves without breaking
the law themselves. Stowe was one of those citizens, and her book, published
2 years after the law was passed, spoke directly to the unjust and inhumane
slave trade.

She also used the book's central female characters to highlight the importance
of motherhood and the role of women as moral anchors in society. The women
assert these roles in the book to help bring about social and political change.
She also recognized the relevance and attractiveness of older women. In one
scene she describes a woman in her late fifties with a face that "time seems to
touch only to brighten and adorn." She goes on to write: "So much has been
said and sung of beautiful young girls, why doesn't somebody wake up to the
beauty of old women?" Most importantly, she created unique depictions of
black women, showing them with Christian values and maternal instincts,
qualities that were typically applied only to their white counterparts. This
quotation comes from the novel's end, where she appeals directly to "mothers
of America"—her white, female, Christian readers.

In our little corner
of the earth [...] the time is
ripely come for alteration
in the laws for women.
And they will be changed.

33

CAROLINE NORTON
1808-1877

SOURCE: *A Letter to the Queen on Lord Chancellor Cranworth's Marriage and Divorce Bill*
DATE: 1855
FIELD: Marriage reform

When English social reformer Caroline Norton wrote an open letter to Queen Victoria in 1855, arguing for a change in English divorce law, it was not her first act of defiance. After separating from her husband in 1836, the author battled him over finances and custody—under the law, all her property belonged to her husband and he could deny her contact with the children. Her pamphlets helped push through the 1839 Custody of Infants Bill, making it possible for separated wives to petition for custody of young children.

When it came to divorce, the law at best ignored women and at worst punished them for their husbands' actions. In her eloquent prose, Norton appealed to the queen's womanhood, explaining to her all the ways the law failed to protect their sex, despite the fact a woman was on the throne: "A married woman in England has no legal existence: her being is absorbed in that of her husband."

Despite her unwavering fight to make change for women, the letter does not paint Norton as an enthusiastic feminist: "The natural position of woman is inferiority to man. Amen!" she exclaims. Whether it was her true opinion, or whether she aimed to subjugate herself in the eyes of the queen, she argued that divorced women be treated under the law the same way as female employees, whose status as workers offered them some protection against exploitation. The Matrimonial Causes Act, passed 2 years later, reflected some of Norton's arguments and granted divorced women the right to receive maintenance, inherit property, and keep possession of their own earnings.

For what is done or learned by one class of women becomes, by virtue of their common womanhood, the property of all women.

34

ELIZABETH BLACKWELL
1821–1910

SOURCE: *Medicine as a Profession for Women* (1860), first delivered as a lecture at Clinton Hall, New York, in 1859
DATE: 1859
FIELDS: Medicine/women in work

"It is not easy to be a pioneer—but oh, it is fascinating," said Elizabeth Blackwell, the first woman to graduate from medical school in the United States. "I would not trade one moment, even the worst moment, for all the riches in the world."

After being rejected from every medical college in New York City and Philadelphia, Blackwell eventually received her degree in medicine from a lesser-known college in 1849 (the male students had voted unanimously to allow her to study there, believing the request to be a joke). Despite proving herself capable in the classroom, no American hospitals were willing to let her practice. She had to return to her native England, from where she had emigrated as a child, and elsewhere in Europe, to gain the necessary experience. She would later become the first woman to have her name entered on the UK's Medical Register of the General Medical Council.

On her return to the USA, Blackwell opened her own clinic in New Jersey and then another with her sister, Emily, called the New York Infirmary for Women and Children. One of the institution's objectives was to "give to poor women the opportunity of consulting physicians of their own sex," something that was unheard of a few years earlier. Having undergone the prejudicial and humiliating experience of being a lone woman in a male medical college, Blackwell went on to cofound the London School of Medicine for Women in England in 1874—the first British school to train women as doctors.

I'd rather be a free spinster and paddle my own canoe.

35

LOUISA MAY ALCOTT
1832–1888

SOURCE: Louisa May Alcott's personal journal
DATE: 1860
FIELDS: Marriage/financial independence

The industrialization of many Western countries in the 19th century continued to challenge the role of women as dependents. In the UK, by the mid-1800s, it is thought that around 40 percent of working-class women contributed wages to their families. In many cases, this gave women more decision-making influence, at home and in their communities. While the bulk of this work was in domestic service, there were new opportunities too in factories and sweatshops—women were seen as a cheaper alternative to mechanization in some sectors. This quotation from American writer Louisa May Alcott, well known for her children's novel *Little Women*, reflects this new spirit of independence. Marriage was no longer the only route to financial security.

She wrote it in her journal, aged 28, 2 years after her older sister Anna, or "Nan," had married: "Saw Nan in her nest, where she and her mate live like a pair of turtle doves. Very sweet and pretty, but I'd rather be a free spinster and paddle my own canoe." And she continued to do just that. Alcott was a suffragist, and the first woman to register to vote in her hometown of Concord, Massachusetts, casting her ballot along with nineteen other women in town elections in 1880. A year previously, she had tried to encourage others to do the same at reading groups she hosted. In 1879 she wrote: "Drove about and drummed up women to my suffrage meeting. So hard to move people out of the old ruts."

What is really wanted in a
woman is that she should be a
permanently pleasant companion.

36

EMILY DAVIES
1830–1921

SOURCE: *The Higher Education of Women*
DATE: 1866
FIELD: Education

Early English feminist Emily Davies is best remembered for her pioneering efforts for women's education. Between 1840 and 1860 in Britain there was a 20 percent rise in literacy among women. New boarding schools, which had previously been exclusively for boys from wealthy families, began to open for girls. The 1880 Education Act, supported with state funding, made education compulsory for all children aged 5–10. However, university education still remained out of reach. There were no residential colleges offering degree-level education to women until Davies, together with a few others, founded Girton College, Cambridge, in 1869.

In an 1866 treatise (quoted opposite), Davies discussed the severe lack of higher education for women, and suggested ways this could be changed and the benefits it could bring to both sexes. She also referred to the swathe of contradictory opinion about the necessity of women's education and its purpose. She quoted a writer who argued that "men are to be pleased, and women are to please," and that women's education should be in service of that. She noted that parents were willing to make sacrifices for their sons' education but not for their daughters'. "A very brief and attenuated course of instruction, beginning late and ending early, is believed to constitute a good and complete education for a woman," she wrote. Despite her best efforts, and some changes in the law, it would take until 1948 for the students of Girton to be considered full members of the university. Ironically, in 1976 it became the first Cambridge women's college to admit men.

I consider it presumption in anyone to pretend to decide what women are or are not, can or cannot be, by natural constitution.

37

JOHN STUART MILL
1806-1873

SOURCE: *The Subjection of Women*
DATE: 1869
FIELD: Equal rights

In the 1800s, one of the principle arguments against women's suffrage was that "the fairer sex" were morally superior to men and that their very nature meant they should remain in the home, under their father or husband's legal care, protected from the harmful influences of the outside world. In 1869, philosopher John Stuart Mill caused much debate after he became the first British man to publicly argue in favor of the emancipation of women. In an eloquent essay titled *The Subjection of Women* he contended that any opposition to the cause was based on prejudice rather than rationality, and that until men and women were treated equally, it was impossible to know if women were more emotional, less politically inclined, and intellectually inferior to men.

Mill's thinking was heavily inspired by his wife, Harriet Taylor Mill, whom he met in 1830 and married in 1851. Mill insisted that his wife had revised all his published writings, and although she died in 1858, many years before he wrote *The Subjection of Women*, in his 1873 autobiography he attributed much of the essay to her, writing: "all that is most striking and profound belongs to my wife." Taylor Mill was also a women's rights advocate, publishing articles about domestic violence and the importance of a woman's right to earn a living. In 1851 she wrote: "A woman who contributes materially to the support of the family, cannot be treated in the same contemptuously tyrannical manner as one who, however she may toil as a domestic drudge, is a dependent on the man for subsistence."

I believe that the influence of woman will save the country before every other power.

38

LUCY STONE
1818–1893

SOURCE: Spoken at the American Equal Rights Association Meeting, New York
DATE: 1869
FIELD: Suffrage

In May 1869, the Fifteenth Amendment to the US Constitution was in the process of being ratified. While it granted suffrage to black men, saying that voting rights could not be denied on account of race, it left women out in the cold. The American Equal Rights Association (AERA), formed 3 years earlier, brought together leaders of the African-American and the women's movements to join their causes and be a larger force for change, but by 1869, the cracks were showing. There was a split in opinion between those demanding suffrage for black men before women, those asking for the reverse, and those wanting both causes to be granted rights simultaneously.

At the 1869 meeting, Frederick Douglass, social reformer and abolitionist, and arguably the most famous black man in the country, spoke in favor of the amendment, saying: "I do not see how anyone can pretend that there is the same urgency in giving the ballot to woman as to the Negro. With us, the matter is a question of life and death." His words received rapturous applause from supporters of the amendment, but the crowd quietened down when Lucy Stone rose to speak. She had been an abolitionist and women's rights advocate most of her 50 years. "We are lost if we turn away from the middle principle and argue for one class," she said, praising the progress the amendment ushered in. And then she said the words opposite, predicting some women would have the vote in 1872. The Nineteenth Amendment, which extended suffrage to women, was not passed until 1920.

It is unjust to punish the sex who are victims of a vice, and leave unpunished the sex who are the main cause.

39

LADIES NATIONAL ASSOCIATION
Est. 1869

SOURCE: "The Women's Protest [against the Contagious Diseases Acts]," *Daily News*
DATE: 1870
FIELDS: Sex work/morality

The signatures of 124 women's rights reformers, including Harriet Martineau, Josephine Butler, and Florence Nightingale, accompanied this 1870 protest statement from the Ladies National Association (LNA). The organization had been set up in the wake of the Contagious Diseases Acts of 1864, 1866, and 1869, which gave the state considerable powers to regulate prostitution in a number of areas in the UK and its colonies, in ways that unfairly discriminated against women. Created because of the high rates of venereal disease in the British military, the law gave police officers the right to detain women and force them to undergo regular medical examinations and long hospital stays.

The cause united women's rights reformers. It was clear to many that women were being unfairly punished, and that the law didn't address the social and moral issues causing the spread of disease. They argued that these measures would not address the health problem. Unlike the more statistically inclined National Association for the Repeal of the Contagious Diseases Act (which failed to include any women in its formation) the LNA considered the moral arguments and the welfare of the women involved. "We consider that liability to arrest, forced treatment, and (where this is resisted) imprisonment with hard labour [...] are punishments of the most degrading kind," the protest statement said. Despite considerable resistance, over almost two decades, the Act wasn't repealed until 1886. The organization continued to fight for equal treatment and the same moral standards for both the sexes, campaigning for the repeal of similar laws in India.

How can "the consent of the governed" be given, if the right to vote be denied?

40

SUSAN B. ANTHONY
1820–1906

SOURCE: "Is It a Crime for a US Citizen to Vote?" speech
DATE: 1873
FIELD: Suffrage

In November 1872, prominent women's rights advocate Susan B. Anthony and fourteen other female suffragists registered to vote in Rochester, New York, in a United States election. They expected to be denied and planned to sue for their right to vote in federal court, but that is not what happened. They registered successfully and went to the polling booth to cast their ballots. Nine days later, they were arrested and charged under the 1870 Enforcement Act for voting "without having a lawful right to vote."

In the run-up to her grand jury trial in June 1873, 53-year-old Anthony embarked on a speaking tour of fifty villages and towns in Monroe and Ontario Counties in an attempt to sway the opinion of potential jurors. She argued that the Declaration of the Independence and the United States Constitution were in place to protect the God-given rights of all people, and that the use of male pronouns meant women were being denied these rights. "I insist if government officials may thus manipulate the pronouns to tax, fine, imprison, and hang women," she said, "women may take the same liberty with them to secure to themselves their right to a voice in the government." Despite her efforts, Anthony was found guilty at trial and sentenced to pay $100, which she refused to do. The suffragists' efforts to gain the vote through the federal courts continued unsuccessfully until 1876, when the National Woman Suffrage Association changed tack and announced its plans to seek a constitutional amendment.

We think it more moral
to prevent the conception of
children than, after they are born,
to murder them by want of
food, air, and clothing.

41

ANNIE BESANT / CHARLES BRADLAUGH
1847–1933 / 1833–1891

SOURCE: *Fruits of Philosophy*
DATE: 1877
FIELD: Birth control

The idea of "voluntary motherhood" versus "involuntary motherhood" emerged in the 1870s. The Neo-Malthusian movement (named for English scholar and economist Thomas Malthus, who wrote about the importance of population control through preventative measures) advocated for increased use of contraceptives and birth control measures to prevent unwanted pregnancies.

British women's rights activist Annie Besant had argued with her husband over family limitation, and it led to their separation. Afterward, she attended London University, and wrote and lectured for the *National Reformer*, a radical activist magazine started by Charles Bradlaugh. They were strongly in favor of the dissemination of information relating to birth control, especially among the working classes, where high infant mortality rates prevailed.

In 1877 Besant and Bradlaugh went on trial after they republished Dr. Charles Knowlton's *Fruits of Philosophy*, an 1832 American book that offered advice on birth control. This quotation appeared in their preface. The book had been on sale in the UK for 44 years, selling 40,000 copies, largely to those who could afford it. When publisher Charles Watts was prosecuted in 1877, pleading guilty to publishing an "obscene" book, the pair of free thinkers were determined to be arrested and tried too, so that they could argue in court for the importance of public access to these types of publications. They even gave the police a helping hand by publishing the location, date, and time they would be selling it for a mere sixpence. Their subsequent trial and guilty verdict (which was quashed on appeal) brought significant attention, with many newspapers reporting on the issue of birth control for the first time.

I would give woman a vote, give her a motive to qualify herself to vote, precisely as I insisted upon giving the colored man the right to vote.

42

FREDERICK DOUGLASS
1818–1895

SOURCE: *Life and Times of Frederick Douglass*
DATE: 1892
FIELDS: Suffrage/abolitionism

The incorporation of the Fifteenth Amendment into the United States Constitution in 1870 left many women feeling that the rights of black American men had usurped their cause and delayed the feminist movement. For black campaigners like Douglass, who had aligned himself early on with the women's rights cause (he was the only African American at the Seneca Falls Convention in 1848, see page 61), it must have been difficult to hear the racially charged rhetoric of former allies like Elizabeth Cady Stanton when the division between the two movements came. Douglass knew that there was barely enough support for an amendment allowing black men the vote, without trying to convince people to let women vote too. In later life, in his autobiography, he remained a staunch supporter of Stanton and continued to unashamedly refer to himself as "a woman's-rights man."

While women's suffrage was still nearly three decades away, he used part of his book to thank those women who had contributed to the abolition of slavery. "When the true history of the anti-slavery cause shall be written," he said, "women will occupy a large space in its pages; for the cause of the slave has been peculiarly a woman's cause." Through his words he continued to speak out in favor of women's rights. With his famed oratorical style, he simply stated: "I have never yet been able to find one consideration, one argument, or suggestion in favour of man's right to participate in civil government which did not equally apply to the right of woman."

43

KATE SHEPPARD
1847–1934

SOURCE: "Is It Right?" in *The Prohibitionist*
DATE: 1892
FIELDS: Suffrage/temperance

In 1893, the British colony of New Zealand became the first self-governing nation to grant the vote to all women over 21 years of age. Suffrage bills had been defeated in the previous 2 years, but after a petition comprising 32,000 women's signatures was delivered to parliament, the government could no longer ignore public opinion. The campaigning that brought about this unprecedented change in the law was spearheaded by Kate Sheppard. A wife, mother, and active member of the Women's Christian Temperance Union (an international social reform and suffrage organization), Sheppard entered the suffrage movement to have greater influence over social reform, particularly liquor prohibition, but the wider cause soon consumed her.

This quotation comes from a longer piece in a temperance journal—one of many pieces of writing by Sheppard that contributed to the success of the women's rights movement. In it she repeated the same question, "Is it right?"

> *Is it right that while the loafer, the gambler, the drunkard, and even the wife-beater has a vote, earnest, educated and refined women are denied it? […]*
> *Is it right that a capable woman, who farms her own land, should be thought unfit to use a vote that is given to the most ignorant of her men servants? […]*
> *Is it right that men should set questions of party above questions of justice?*

New Zealand's suffragists' success had a significant impact on the neighboring British colonies of South Australia and Western Australia, which passed universal suffrage in 1894 and 1899 respectively. Sheppard and her contemporaries became sought-after speakers in the USA and the UK.

There is no female mind.
The brain is not an organ of sex.

As well speak of a female liver.

CHARLOTTE PERKINS GILMAN
1860–1935

SOURCE: *Women and Economics: The Economic Factor Between Men and Women as a Factor in Social Evolution*
DATE: 1898
FIELD: Social theory

In the latter part of the 19th century and early 1900s, with the vote still not won in many of the world's largest democracies, feminist theorists were also focused on the changing role of women in society—perhaps none more so than Charlotte Perkins Gilman, one of the most influential American feminist thinkers of the period. Gilman suffered from mental-health issues, triggered by an unhappy marriage. After recovering from a breakdown and taking the radical step to divorce, she moved from the East Coast to California and began writing widely about women's issues. She also embarked on lecture tours across the country and in the UK. She was appalled by the domestic servitude of wives and mothers, believing instead that women should work outside the home and that housekeeping chores should be done by paid professionals. She also advocated for communal childcare and for boys and girls to be raised identically.

In Gilman's mind, the idea of gendered roles for men and women was outdated, especially when it came to the jobs women could do, for how long they could do them, and the clothes they should wear. She also believed childcare should be split between parents—she sent her own daughter to live with her ex-husband while she went on tour. These revolutionary views were imbued throughout her work, from her 1892 short story, *The Yellow Wallpaper*, about a woman's nervous breakdown caused by confinement, to her 1898 treatise, *Women and Economics*, from which comes the well-known quotation opposite, to her later utopian works.

I told him the
chief product
of the women
had been the
men.

ANNA HOWARD SHAW
1847–1919

SOURCE: Speech to the National Woman's Suffrage Association
DATE: 1899
FIELD: Suffrage

Anna Howard Shaw had a background as a Methodist preacher and became a trained physician, but it was during her medical studies that she found her true calling. She became acquainted with Lucy Stone and her husband Henry Blackwell (brother of Elizabeth Blackwell, see page 73) and with them became immersed in the women's suffrage movement. Shaw was known as a sharp wit and engaging speaker, and it was at the National American Woman Suffrage Association's (NAWSA) 1899 convention that she made this clever retort. She explained how a gentleman opposed to the enfranchisement of women had once said to her: "Women have never produced anything of any value to the world." She told him "the chief product of the women had been the men, and left it to him to decide whether the product was of any value."

In 1904, she succeeded Susan B. Anthony as president of NAWSA. At the start of her presidency, only four states had granted full suffrage to women, while elsewhere women were able to vote in municipal elections and for school boards, for example. Under Shaw's leadership, the number of suffrage workers rose considerably, as did the number of organized campaigns and expenditure. By the time she resigned from the post in 1915, twelve states had granted full suffrage, including Washington and California, and the tide was turning. Shaw passed away on July 3, 1919, one month after the US Senate voted in favor of the Woman Suffrage Amendment.

We have secured
the strength and
the right to fight!
Our great work is
only beginning.

46

LOUISA LAWSON
1848–1920

SOURCE: *The Dawn*
DATE: 1902
FIELDS: Suffrage/journalism

The Dawn: A Journal for Australian Women was the brainchild of a penniless single
mother who had pulled herself out of poverty and an abusive marriage. In
Sydney, Louisa Lawson founded the magazine, which was staffed and produced
entirely by women, and it soon became an important mouthpiece for the
women's suffrage movement, with 1,000 subscribers. She also started the
Dawn Club, a fortnightly meeting for women to discuss their ideas, debate,
and practice their public-speaking skills.

Women had been granted voting rights in two of the six federating colonies in
the last years of the 19th century. When the Commonwealth of Australia was
formed in 1901, these rights were retained, and with the passing of the
Commonwealth Franchise Act (1902) the right to vote in federal elections was
granted to: "all persons not under twenty-one years of age, whether male or
female, married or unmarried." It also stipulated that they be "natural-born or
naturalized subjects of the King," meaning British subjects.

It was in the wake of this change in the law that Lawson delivered the quotation
opposite. "The redemption of the world is in the hands of women," she
continued, "and there is no power so potent for purification as the influence
of woman!" Perhaps the fight Lawson was referring to was the change that still
needed to come—despite having the right to stand in federal elections, women
were not elected on a national level until 1943, and indigenous women were
denied the right to vote in federal elections for another 60 years.

We no longer want to be treated as [...] helpless creatures begging men for protection.

47

TAMPERE BRANCH OF LEAGUE OF WORKING WOMEN
Est. 1900

SOURCE: *Tampereen naisten vaatimukset äänioikeus- ja eduskunta-asiassa (Women in Tampere: Women's Voting Rights and Parliamentary Affairs)*
DATE: 1907
FIELDS: Workers' rights/equal rights

The start of the 20th century brought significant gains for women's rights movements across Europe. In 1906, Finland became the first country to grant universal suffrage to all people, including the right to stand for office. The suffrage movement in Finland coincided with a rise in workers' rights protests, sparked by Czarist Russia's restrictions to the autonomy it had previously allowed its Finnish dominion to maintain. At the time, most working-class people were excluded from voting. The elitist parties called for suffrage to be extended only to wealthy women, while the newly formed Workers Party wanted full suffrage, regardless of gender, wealth, or nationality.

In October 1905, a week-long general strike, known as the Great Strike, saw Finland come to a standstill. Members of the League of Working Women, made up largely of domestic servants, also participated in the strike—much to their bourgeois employers' horror—and attended special women's suffrage meetings. After the strike ended, a year of further action, and the threat of a second general strike, eventually led to the change in the law. For one day of mass demonstrations, the League wrote a "National Women's Declaration," in which they contrasted the labor contribution of women in society with their lack of political rights. The Tampere branch expanded on this with the quotation opposite. They wanted to be treated as "comrades in battle, free women of a free people, willing to bear all the consequences, whether they be light or heavy, that the future may weigh upon our nation's shoulders."

If I had
the right to legislate,
I would decree [...]

48

BAHITHAT AL-BADIYA
1886–1918

SOURCE: *Al-Nisa'iyat*
DATE: 1909
FIELD: Suffrage

As feminism found a voice in Finland in the wave of anti-colonial sentiment, in the Middle East there was a growing resistance to foreign and local domination, which brought with it a hunger for the emancipation of women. From the second half of the 19th century, these ideas were propagated by great thinkers, who wrote about the need to rid the Arab world of the injustices imposed upon women, such as the practice of plural marriage, female slavery, and concubinage (the right of men to have sexual intercourse with their slaves). Arab women were heavily involved in the movement from the start, particularly through their journalism and poetry.

Malak Hefni Nassef, who went by the pen name Bahithat al-Badiya ("searcher of the desert"), was one of the first Egyptian women to advocate openly for women's rights. In this 1909 lecture to a group of women at the Umma Party Club, she expressed her desire to have a say in various aspects of life. She wanted primary and secondary school education for girls, a quota for women in medicine and education, and for a woman to be able to meet the man she was betrothed to before marriage. Two years later, she presented her list of modest demands to the Egyptian Congress; they were all rejected. Yet the forthrightness of Al-Badiya's writing paved the way for more radical feminist ideas and activism. In 1923, Hoda Shaarawi, famous for a public demonstration in which she and a number of other women removed their veils at Cairo's main train station, founded the Egyptian Feminist Union—the basis for future feminist victories in the region.

Motherhood can be sacred only when it is voluntary.

49

CICELY HAMILTON
1872–1952

SOURCE: *Marriage as a Trade*
DATE: 1909
FIELDS: Marriage/motherhood

Cicely Hamilton's words, "Motherhood can be sacred only when it is voluntary, when a child is desired by a woman who feels herself fit to bear and rear it," reflected the UK's growing voluntary motherhood movement among what are now referred to as first-wave feminists (the feminists of the 19th and early 20th centuries). Although there was disagreement as to how this should be achieved—through the use of abstinence and "natural" preventative methods, or through the use of contraception—moral reformers, suffragists, and those in support of a more liberal attitude to women's sexuality were all in agreement: involuntary mothers were oppressed by child-rearing.

Hamilton's book explored the business of marriage in a wider context too. She argued that women's intellectual development was being severely impaired by the fact that they were raised to seek out successful marriages above all else. She recognized that as more and more women found their way to the workplace, the comradeship and companionship they found had unleashed a new power. If women's wages were to increase above basic subsistence levels, she wrote, and if they were to be anything more than "hewers of wood, drawers of water, and unthinking reproducers of our kind" they had to stand together.

Hamilton, an actress and playwright, was a founding member of the Women Writers' Suffrage League and wrote a number of propaganda plays, including 1909's *How the Vote Was Won*, in which the government denies women the vote on the basis that they are taken care of by men, leading all the working women to down tools and insist on support from their male relatives.

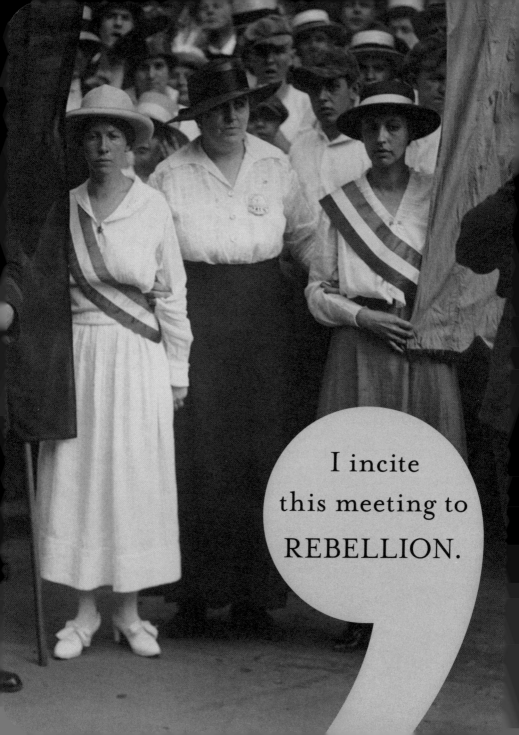

50

EMMELINE PANKHURST
1858–1928

SOURCE: Speech at the Royal Albert Hall, London
DATE: October 17, 1912
FIELD: Suffrage

In the UK, some suffragists were growing impatient with the political efforts of the largely middle-class National Union of Women's Suffrage Societies. In 1903, Emmeline Pankhurst, together with her daughters Christabel and Sylvia, started a new organization: The Women's Social and Political Union. They believed it was important to include the working-class in their struggle and that more extreme action was needed. The organization's motto was "deeds not words." The *Daily Mail* newspaper christened them "the suffragettes."

The suffragettes used radical methods to bring attention to their cause, in many cases breaking the law and facing harsh prison sentences. Once imprisoned, they would go on hunger strike, and force feeding was common. It was shocking to see women being treated this way so publicly, and their rough treatment won the cause more public support.

Proposals for changes to the law in 1912, which would give all men the right to vote but explicitly ignored women, added fuel to the fire. The government warned that militant action would not result in the enfranchisement of women. This was the year that Pankhurst gave one of her most famous speeches at London's Royal Albert Hall (a common venue for women's rights speeches and conferences). "Be militant each in your own way," she told the crowd not long after she had been released from prison. "Take me if you dare," she challenged the government. The speech had the desired effect, and the violence escalated, such that in 1913 the Women's Social and Political Union became the first political organization to be banned from the Royal Albert Hall.

Once our eyes are open, **we** cannot fall asleep again.

51

RAICHŌ HIRATSUKA
1886–1971

SOURCE: *Seitō* magazine
DATE: 1913
FIELD: Feminist literature

"Once our eyes are open, we cannot fall asleep again. We are alive. We are
awake," wrote Raichō Hiratsuka in a 1913 edition of *Seitō* (Bluestocking)
magazine. Titled "To the Women of the World," this was one of the most
famous articles to appear in Japan's first all-women literary publication. It was
founded by Hiratsuka and five other women who were members of the feminist
Bluestocking Society. The magazine ran from 1911 to 1916 and included
classical haiku, poetry, impressionistic essays, and dramatic criticism. It also
featured translated works by radical Western authors like Russian-American
anarchist Emma Goldman and Swedish suffragist Ellen Key. Women were
allowed to submit 10 pages to the magazine in place of a membership fee,
giving less wealthy women access to important feminist material.

While the struggle for women's rights and suffrage was being fought and
won in some parts of the world, in Japan, women were still tightly bound by
a patriarchal culture that saw women as subordinates to men. By its second
year, the magazine's writers were using the platform to probe their
own society, which condoned adultery in men but could imprison women
for up to 2 years for the same behavior. It covered abortion, prostitution, birth
control, and marriage, and helped to promote women's issues to a wider
audience. *Seitō*'s popularity (at its peak it sold 3,000 copies per month),
proved that, despite appearances, there were many Japanese women unsatisfied
with the hand they had been dealt. Japanese women only received the right to
vote in 1945, influenced by American occupation following World War Two.

I MYSELF HAVE NEVER BEEN ABLE TO FIND OUT WHAT FEMINISM IS; I ONLY KNOW THAT PEOPLE CALL ME A FEMINIST WHENEVER I EXPRESS SENTIMENTS THAT DIFFERENTIATE ME FROM A DOORMAT OR A PROSTITUTE.

52

REBECCA WEST

1892–1983

SOURCE: "Mr Chesterton in Hysterics: A Study in Prejudice," *Clarion*
DATE: 1913
FIELD: Social commentary

As the term "feminism" was not used regularly until the late 1800s, the first-wave feminists who grew up with it were the first to claim it and define it, often in the face of negative connotations. Born in 1892, Rebecca West is considered to be one of the greatest writers of her generation; feminism and social reform played a huge role in her life. She started her literary career in 1911, writing for radical feminist journal, *The Freewoman*, just 2 years before she made the caustic statement opposite. It was in response to an article by English writer G. K. Chesterton, in which he criticized Dorothy Montefiore—an English-Australian suffragist who had been part of a plan to relocate Dublin children to England and Belfast during the workers' strikes of 1913. Chesterton used Montefiore's gender against her, arguing she was part of a feminist movement that was like "an idolatrous procession cutting across and stopping the march of modern men in revolt."

West's statement was characteristic of her spirited and independent approach to writing. No one was safe from her critical eye, women especially; she made fun of suffragists and her gender, whom she argued spent too much time and energy on falling in love and relationships. Yet it was the most esteemed male writers, like Chesterton, for whom she reserved her brutal wit. At 19, she described celebrated author H. G. Wells as "the old maid among novelists." She later had a 10-year relationship and a child with him.

When men once get the habit [to vote], who knows where it will end? It is hard enough to keep them at home now!

53

NELLIE McCLUNG
1873–1951

SOURCE: From Nellie Mcclung's fictional retelling of "The Women's Parliament" in *Purple Springs*, based on her speech given at the Walker Theatre, Winnipeg
DATE: 1914
FIELD: Women's suffrage

Women's rights campaigner Nellie McClung was integral to the change in suffrage laws in her native Canada. She became one of the most prominent voices of a relatively peaceful movement—her traditional viewpoints about female morality and motherhood made her palatable to both conservatives and liberals. Women's voting rights varied across the country and from city to city as suffragists initially focused their efforts on municipal and school-board elections. Opposition to provincial election rights was strongest in the east, while the newly colonized western provinces were more receptive (in part due to the need to attract women to help populate these regions). The farming community, in particular, was extremely influential in endorsing women's suffrage in Manitoba.

In 1914, the Winnipeg Political Equality League—a group of activists intent on changing conditions for female factory workers—presented "The Women's Parliament," a mock legislature in which men petitioned women for the vote. The women "politicians" sat on the stage of Winnipeg's Walker Theatre. McClung, a league organizer, took the leadership role and openly mocked Manitoba Premier Rodmond Roblin over three sold-out shows. She employed the same patronizing language used by male politicians, opening her remarks by complimenting the men in the audience on their appearance. "Oh, no, man is made for something higher and better than voting," she said. "The trouble is that if men start to vote, they will vote too much." In 1916, Manitoba became the first province to grant women the right to vote and hold office.

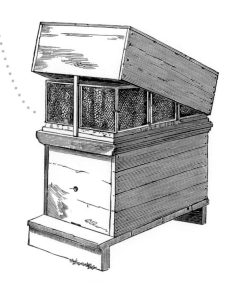

Honeyed phrases are pleasant
to listen to, but the sensible
women of our country would
prefer more substantial gifts.

54

REBECCA FELTON
1835-1930

SOURCE: From the speech "Why I Am a Suffragist" given in Cartersville, Georgia
DATE: 1915
FIELD: Women's suffrage

The first two decades of the 20th century saw women's suffrage introduced in a number of American states, but the situation in the South was somewhat different. There was huge antisuffrage sentiment there, particularly from big business, which relied on cheap child labor and lower wages for women, and from career politicians, who held sway over the male vote.

However, there were suffragists there too, like Rebecca Felton, an *Atlanta Journal* columnist who spearheaded the women's rights movement in Georgia. Like many white southern women, she was outraged that black men were legally allowed to vote while she wasn't (although the law failed to protect any who dared show up at the polling stations). In this 1915 speech she spoke about all the ways state laws had mistreated her gender over the years, and how the southern gentleman had failed to give the "substantial gift" of voting rights to the very women he routinely praised.

In 1919, Georgia became the first state to reject the Nineteenth Amendment, also known as the Susan B. Anthony Amendment (after the suffrage leader), which stated that a person couldn't be denied the right to vote on account of their sex. Georgia wouldn't formally ratify the amendment until 1970. Felton fared slightly better. In 1922, at the age of eighty-seven, she became the first woman to be sworn in as a United States Senator, serving in that official capacity for one day before her elected replacement took office. In her only speech to the Senate, she looked to a future when women with "ability [...] integrity of purpose [and] unstinted usefulness" would follow in her footsteps.

No woman can call herself free

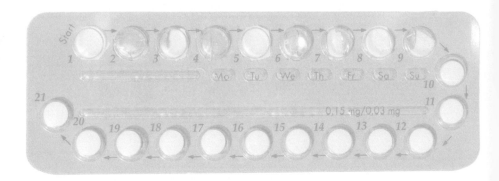

who does not own and control her body.

55

MARGARET SANGER
1879–1966

SOURCE: *Woman and the New Race*
DATE: 1920
FIELD: Reproductive rights

In recent years, Margaret Sanger's support of eugenics—a popular movement in the 1920s and 1930s to improve humankind through selective breeding—has overshadowed the essential work she did in support of women's reproductive rights in the United States. She opened the first birth control clinic in Brooklyn, New York, in 1916, only for it to be shut down nine days later. She was arrested and charged with crimes related to sharing information about birth control. The judge offered to go lightly on her, if she promised to end her efforts, but she refused and received a 30-day jail sentence (during which she used her birth control knowledge to educate her fellow inmates).

In 1920 she published her first book, *Woman and the New Race* (referring to the new human race), in which she told women to believe in themselves and their own ability to make change happen. In one chapter on birth control she said, "The basic freedom of the world is woman's freedom. A free race cannot be born of slave mothers." She recognized the correlation between poverty and abortion rates—which were highest among poor married women who did not have access to information about birth control methods. These women faced the choice between "forced maternity" or an illegal, and oftentimes dangerous, abortion. Sanger continued to fight for women's access to contraception, opening a research center in Manhattan to collect statistics about birth control methods and then, in 1921, founding the American Birth Control League, which would later be known as Planned Parenthood.

Now women have equal rights, but we are only equal on paper.

56

ELIZABETH SELBERT
1896-1986

SOURCE: SPD Women's Conference, Kassel, Germany
DATE: 1920
FIELD: Equal rights

Article 109 of the Weimar Constitution of 1919 stated: "All Germans are equal before the law. Men and women have the same fundamental civil rights and duties." The country's new constitution also stated that men and women over the age of twenty had the right to vote. The groundwork of 19th-century campaigners, like Louise Otto-Peters (see page 63), the activities of the International Women's Suffrage Alliance (founded in Berlin in 1904), and the efforts of feminists during the November Revolution of 1918–1919 had finally come to fruition. During the years of the Weimar Republic (1919–1933) the majority of voters were women, and in the first year they were entitled to do so, 82 percent of women voters showed up to the ballots. Not only that, but women candidates held 10 percent of the seats in the Reichstag (parliament).

Social Democratic Party (SPD) member Elisabeth Selbert was right to be skeptical when she made this statement at a women's conference a year later. Those rights were soon challenged by the rise of the Nazi Party. In 1934, Adolf Hitler reinforced his party's stance on women's main role in society: "Woman's world is her husband, her family, her children, her house." After World War Two, Selbert, by then a qualified lawyer and elected member of the State Consultative Assembly, was one of sixty-five people chosen to formulate a new constitution for Germany. She made it her mission to ensure that the wording from the Weimar Constitution was included and enforced, making it necessary for the law to change to reflect these basic rights.

Now at last
we can begin.

57

CRYSTAL EASTMAN
1891-1928

SOURCE: "Now We Can Begin," *The Liberator*
DATE: 1920
FIELD: Women's suffrage

On June 4, 1919, the United States Senate passed the Nineteenth Amendment to the Constitution, granting women the right to vote. The law required that for an amendment to be adopted, thirty-six states had to ratify it. By March, 1920, thirty-five had done so, but the majority of the southern states had rejected it. The final decision fell to Tennessee's state legislators on August 18, 1920, to decide whether women would finally receive the sought-after right to vote across the country. And the casting vote that ratified the amendment was Harry Burn's, a 24-year-old Republican senator, whose mother had asked him to "be a good boy" and vote in favor.

Shortly after the Nineteenth Amendment was certified on August 26, 1920, Crystal Eastman, a lawyer and co-founder of the National Woman's Party, published an essay, in which she considered what would come next for women's rights campaigners. She wrote about rearranging the world so that women could exercise their skills in a variety of ways, rather than being restricted to the realms of homemaking and childcare; about breaking down the remaining barriers, legal and otherwise, that prevented women from succeeding in all professions; about eradicating inequality in pay; and about voluntary motherhood and state benefits for those who chose to have children. The vote was key to making significant changes in all these areas, and while the battle to win it had been long, the war for women's rights was only just beginning. On November 2, 1920, more than eight million women voted in federal elections for the first time.

Social advance depends
as much upon the process
through which it is secured
as upon the result itself.

58

JANE ADDAMS
1860-1935

SOURCE: *Peace and Bread in Time of War*
DATE: 1922
FIELD: Pacifist feminism

The majority of feminist groups supported the "Great War" efforts in their own countries—it was a chance to display their patriotism and persuade lawmakers to vote for suffrage. Yet in neutral countries, or those that were yet to enter the fray, the chance for pacifist feminist views to be heard was greater. Three thousand women gathered in Washington, DC, in 1915 for the founding of the Woman's Peace Party—Jane Addams was among them. Later that year she traveled to The Hague in the Netherlands, where she chaired the Women's Congress. All delegates had to pledge their support for women's suffrage, something the organizers saw as inseparable from their objective: to end the war and restore peace. Their twenty proposals included the right of self-determination for all and the creation of an international authority to arbitrate in disputes between nations. Despite their efforts, women's views were marginal in the peace negotiations that took place in Paris in 1919. Few world leaders wished to see gender equality, which they regarded as a matter for national debate, mixed up with the international agreement for peace.

Jane Addams dedicated her life to social activism, particularly to international peacekeeping. She served as president of the Women's International League for Peace and Freedom (born out of the 1915 Women's Congress) and helped provide food and supplies to women and children in Europe affected by the war. She was awarded the Nobel Peace Prize (the second of sixteen women to have received it) in 1931 for her efforts.

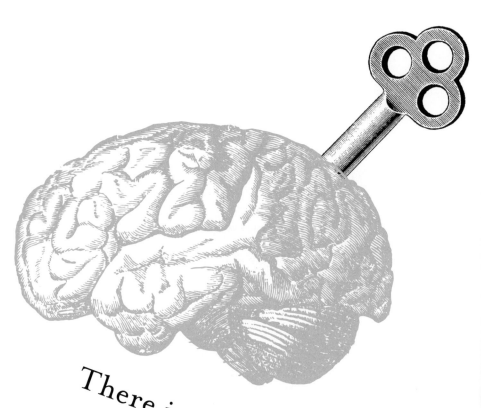

There is no gate, no lock,
no bolt that you can set upon
the freedom of my mind.

59

VIRGINIA WOOLF
1882–1941

SOURCE: *A Room of One's Own*
DATE: 1928
FIELD: Women in literature

Virginia Woolf's 1928 essay, *A Room of One's Own*, is now considered a key 20th-century feminist text. It was inspired by a talk given to the students of Cambridge's two women's colleges about women in fiction. The essay, which was published shortly after, touched on the titular idea of a woman needing both money (£500 in Woolf's opinion, thought to be about $37,000 in today's money) and a dedicated space (the room) to work as a writer. The wider discussion and semi-fictional encounters in the book covered a number of issues and ideas central to Woolf's feminism: the educational and financial disparities between the sexes, the detrimental effect on society of women's exclusion from creative and political domains, and what was the first, albeit brief, literary history of women writers, in which she explores her predecessors, their creativity, and the constraints they faced.

The radical text also incorporates attitudes toward women's education at the time. While Cambridge's first two women's colleges were founded in 1869 and 1871 respectively, there was still serious opposition to women's inclusion in the country's leading educational institutions. "Any transient visitor to this planet," she wrote, "could not fail to be aware that England is under the rule of the patriarchy." Above all, the text was a call to women to take up the pen and write.

I PERSONALLY LOVE THIS PROFESSION AND, IF EVER POSSIBLE, I ALSO WANT TO PRACTICE IT.

60

REGINA JONAS
1902-1944

SOURCE: "May a Woman Hold Rabbinic Office?"
DATE: 1930
FIELD: Theology

In 1924, Regina Jonas enrolled at Berlin's College for Jewish Studies. While there were other female students at this liberal institute, working toward their teacher's degrees, Jonas had a different plan. She was hoping to be ordained as a rabbi, and so become the first woman to do so.

Her 1930 thesis dealt with the controversy at the heart of her plan. In it, she posited that a female rabbinate was part of Jewish tradition and was based in Jewish law, in opposition to both Orthodox and Reform points of view at the time. She concluded that it was nothing but prejudice and ignorance that stood in the way of a woman becoming a rabbi. In contrast with the more liberal views of many Jews today, and despite the Torah's instruction "to be fruitful and multiply," Jonas felt that women rabbis should not marry and that their suitability for the rabbinate was in part because of "female qualities," such as compassion and social skills. Despite her persuasive argument, Jonas graduated as a religious teacher, not a rabbi. She had to wait until 1935 to finally be ordained.

With the war approaching, she was only able to pursue her calling for a few years. She traveled around Germany, preaching in the liberal synagogues, many of whose former rabbis had been imprisoned or had emigrated, and visiting the Jewish sick and elderly, who were facing dire circumstances. Even when she was deported to Theresienstadt concentration camp in 1942, she continued to work there as a rabbi. On October 12, 1944, Jonas was transported to Auschwitz with her mother. It is believed they were murdered on the same day.

To call woman the weaker sex is a libel;
it is man's injustice to woman.

MAHATMA GANDHI
1869–1948

SOURCE: *Young India*
DATE: 1930
FIELD: Nonviolent protest

Mahatma Gandhi claimed that he learned his nonviolent passive resistance approach from the women around him—his wife and mother in particular. He also made efforts to combat sexual discrimination, recognizing that Indian women were suppressed by the country's laws and customs, particularly child marriage, the purdah (veil), and the dowry system. He actively encouraged women to leave the confines of their homes and join him to protest for India's independence through his satyagraha philosophy (a form of nonviolent civil resistance). He appealed to them directly, noting their empathetic and sacrificial nature, and their ability to withstand great hardship. Millions of women from all parts of society were part of the movement. They risked their lives and the threat of harsh jail terms to help bring independence to their nation.

However, it is important to note that while Gandhi preached about equality, including women in his protests, he also held nonfeminist views about menstruation, rape, and female sexuality—a social legacy that still prevails and impacts the lives of Indian women today. He was a strong believer in monogamy, seeing sexual relations solely as an act of procreation. When he met Margaret Sanger (see page 115), a fierce advocate of contraceptive rights for women, while she was touring India in the 1930s, he told her, "It becomes a lustful thing when you take love for your own satisfaction." Drawing the comparison with the health problems that arise from food and alcohol, he asked, "Would it not be better not to take the chocolate or whisky?"

Women must try to do things as men have tried. When they fail, their failure must be but a challenge to others.

62

AMELIA EARHART
1897–1937

SOURCE: In a letter to her husband George Putnam
DATE: 1937
FIELD: Aviation

By the 1930s, women in the Western world were enjoying growing political and educational freedom—in Britain they gained equal voting rights with men in 1928, and the Education Acts of 1902 and 1918 meant more women were attending school than ever before. Sex discrimination legislation also meant it became easier for women to enter professions from which they had previously been barred.

In the USA, Amelia Earhart became a record-setting aviation pioneer who more than matched the daring of her male equivalents. Between 1928 and 1937, she became the first woman to fly across the Atlantic, and then the first woman to do it solo, as well as the first person to fly from Hawaii to California, from Mexico City to Los Angeles, and from Mexico City to New York. For Earhart and other female flyers, aviation offered something beyond the restrictions of everyday life, in which women were still expected to behave, think, and look a certain way. And for their efforts they earned respect, recognition, and worldwide fame.

Earhart married in 1931 but remained committed to her career, writing in a letter to her soon-to-be husband George Putnam, "Please let us not interfere with the other's work or play." It was in May 1937, in another letter to Putnam, while preparing for an equatorial round-the-world flight that she wrote the words opposite, prefacing them with: "Please know that I am quite aware of the hazards. I want to do it because I want to do it." It would be her last flight. Her plane went missing somewhere in the South Pacific and was never found.

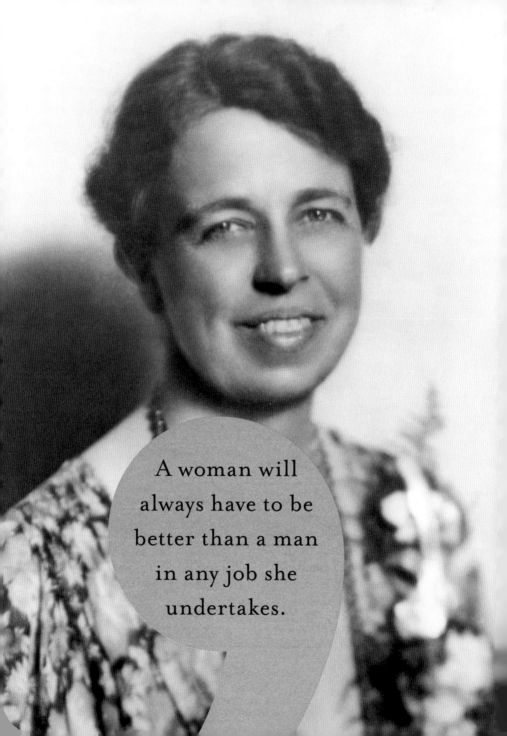

A woman will always have to be better than a man in any job she undertakes.

63

ELEANOR ROOSEVELT
1884-1962

SOURCE: "My Day"
DATE: 1945
FIELD: Politics

Eleanor Roosevelt became the most active first lady in American history
when her husband, Franklin D. Roosevelt (FDR), passed away suddenly from
a massive cerebral hemorrhage. She had traveled abroad with the president,
visiting troops during World War Two, and established the weekly press
conferences held at the White House (although she only allowed women
reporters to attend). Her husband had steered the nation through the storms
of the Great Depression and most of the war. He was succeeded by his vice-
president, Harry S. Truman, who had big shoes to fill.

From 1935 to 1962 Eleanor Roosevelt wrote a six-day-a-week column, "My
Day," which was nationally syndicated, appearing in 90 papers at the height
of its popularity. The column was unprecedented for a first lady and explored
issues such as women in the workplace and equal rights. Her husband's death
didn't stop her sharing her views with the country. When President Truman,
who had promised to continue his predecessor's politics, got rid of two-thirds
of the cabinet, preferring to choose his own people, there was one dismissal
that bothered Roosevelt in particular. Labor Secretary Frances Perkins was
the first woman member of a United States presidential cabinet when she was
appointed by FDR in 1933. Truman asked her to serve on the Civil Service
Commission, but it was undoubtedly a step down. Roosevelt praised Perkins'
work record, writing the quote opposite. "There is no woman in the cabinet
today," she bemoaned, "but there will be again in the future."

Here it is,
my sisters.

64

EVA PERÓN
1919-1952

SOURCE: From a speech given from the Casa Rosada in
Buenos Aires, Argentina
DATE: 1947
FIELDS: Politics/women's suffrage

On September 23, 1947, Argentina's first lady, Eva Perón, stepped out
onto the balcony of the Casa Rosada—the executive mansion and office of her
husband President Juan Perón—and addressed the crowds gathered in the Plaza
de Mayo. "Here it is, my sisters," she said, referring to a short document, a law
only seven articles long, that had been approved by the National Congress a few
weeks earlier, and signed that day by her husband and the interior minister.
Article one stated "Argentine women will have the same political rights as men
and will be subjected to the same obligations provided or imposed by the law to
Argentine men." Not only did the law give women the right to vote, but also the
right to be elected to office.

Evita, as she was affectionately known, declared it "a victory for women over the
denial, misunderstanding, and vested interests of the hierarchy, cast off by our
national awakening." The first lady had been instrumental in fighting for
women's suffrage during her husband's first presidential term. While some
argue her feminism was a political strategy to secure more future votes for her
husband, she worked tirelessly to include women in the political arena as well
as championing the rights of the working classes.

Four years later, in 1951, four million Argentine women went to the polls,
helping to deliver Juan Perón a landslide victory. Among them was Eva, who
voted for the first and final time that year—she died of cervical cancer in 1952.
After her husband's reelection she was officially declared "Spiritual Leader of
the Nation."

One is
not born, but
rather becomes
a woman.

65

SIMONE DE BEAUVOIR
1908–1986

SOURCE: *The Second Sex*
DATE: 1949
FIELD: Equality

World War Two and the economic boom that followed it brought more and more women into the workplace. With more education and a more widely recognized role in society came a wider appreciation of the inequities they faced within it, both economically and socially. French author and philosopher Simone de Beauvoir's powerful words from her widely read and celebrated book *The Second Sex* gave birth to a new, modern feminism, a reflection and a precursor of this struggle for equality. In it she explored the unsavory parameters of female freedom, the entrenched beliefs about femininity, and the flawed traditional relationship between the sexes, which she believed had to be confronted for true liberation to blossom.

The book asked many questions women are still contending with today—issues surrounding the sense of agency over sexuality, the demands of housework and motherhood, and the constant struggle between one's professional interests and personal life. Beauvoir looked at all of this through an existential lens, arguing that one is not born a woman, but becomes one, as society reacts with hostility to each stage of a girl "becoming flesh"—her body no longer her own but something for others to gawk at, comment on, or touch without permission. She argued that the biological condition of being a woman was not necessarily a disadvantage, but that a patriarchal society's antagonistic and domineering attitude toward it made it so.

Beauvoir never married or had children—her legacy was her words. Despite being published nearly 70 years ago, parts of this groundbreaking feminist work are as relevant and resonant today as they were in 1949.

NO ONE WILL DELIVER FREEDOM TO WOMEN, EXCEPT WOMAN HERSELF.

66

DORIA SHAFIK
1908-1975

SOURCE: *Al-Ahram* newspaper
DATE: 1951
FIELDS: Militancy/women's rights

These words opposite were written shortly before scholar and activist Doria Shafik set out on February 19, 1951, with 1,500 other women, to storm the Egyptian parliament. "The freedom granted so far remained on the surface of our social structure," she wrote, "leaving intact the manacles which bound the hands of the Egyptian women."

Since Hoda Shaarawi founded the Egyptian Feminist Union in 1923 (see page 101), the women's rights movement had grown in prominence in the region, although it still largely remained the domain of the wealthy and educated. It was a movement Shafik had been part of since her teenage years. She founded a journal in 1945, *Bint Al-Nil* (*Daughters of the Nile*), with the aim of educating women, who still had no role in the political arena. In it she advocated equal pay, the right to vote, literacy, an end to polygamy, and divorce law reform. In 1948 *Bint Al-Nil* adopted a more militant approach.

In 1951, at a time of great resistance to British involvement in Egypt, Shafik used the tactics of her nationalist brothers to bring about change. Together with other activists, she forced her way into parliament and boisterously demonstrated for four hours, publicly defying the male authorities that surrounded them and bringing international press attention to their cause. This protest and those that followed, including a 1954 hunger strike, eventually led to change for Egyptian women. Although there were still stipulations placed on women's voting that did not apply to men, the 1956 constitution gave women the right to vote and run for office.

Whatever women do they must do twice as well as men to be thought half as good.

67

CHARLOTTE WHITTON
1896-1975

SOURCE: *Canada Month*
DATE: 1963
FIELD: Politics

Charlotte Whitton was the mayor of Ottawa from 1951 to 1956 and then
again from 1960 to 1964, making her the first woman to be mayor of a major
Canadian city. In 1951, when the incumbent mayor died suddenly of a heart
attack, there were hardly any female politicians at any level of Canadian
government. Whitton, who had spent most of her career thus far as a prominent
social- and child-welfare advocate, took on the challenge of running for the
Ottawa Local Council of Women. Her election victory was a shock to the
patriarchal "old boys club" of Canadian politics, but her mayoral years were
not smooth sailing. Her political style was considered brash and pugnacious
(she famously took a swing at a fellow council member for a sexist remark),
and she held controversial views on immigration, support programs, and
divorce reform.

However, Whitton was a fervent supporter of women's rights—she criticized the
double standard that unfairly blamed unmarried women for pregnancies but
not the babies' fathers; she was a fierce proponent of other women running for
government; and she believed in equal pay for equal work, a view that was
considered controversial at the time. She was an early believer in the idea of a
"living wage," so that all employees could provide for their dependents. Her
negative public image, which was in large part perpetuated by the press, was
indicative of the heavy criticism that women in politics had to face. Their every
decision, comment, and lifestyle choice was critiqued far beyond those of their
male contemporaries.

Is this all?

68

BETTY FRIEDAN
1921-2006

SOURCE: *The Feminine Mystique*
DATE: 1963
FIELD: Gender roles

In 1957, American freelance journalist Betty Friedan conducted a survey of her fellow female alumni at a Smith College reunion. The material would go on to form the basis of *The Feminine Mystique*, the bestselling nonfiction book in the USA in 1963 (the first paperback print run sold 1.4 million copies). In it, she addressed "the problem that has no name"—the widespread unhappiness of suburban housewives, who had abandoned education and professional pursuits and now found themselves unfulfilled by domesticity, anesthetized by the advertising for shiny new appliances. In the opening paragraph, she posited that suburban housewives were all struggling alone as they made beds, bought groceries, and chauffeured their children to various activities. And as each of those women "lay beside her husband at night—she was afraid to ask even of herself the silent question—'Is this all?'"

Friedan's book has since been widely criticized for attacking motherhood and the choice to be a homemaker, as well as for ignoring the radically different experiences of working-class and nonwhite women, who often had no choice but to work long hours as well as taking care of children and a home. However, it has also been credited with rallying huge swathes of middle-class American women and igniting a "second wave" of feminism. The book is widely regarded as one of the most influential of the 20th century and has sold more than three million copies. Friedan would go on to set up and become the first president of the National Organization for Women (NOW) and would continue to inspire generations of feminists up until her death, at age 85, in 2006.

In politics, if you want anything said, ask a man. If you want anything done, ask a woman.

69

MARGARET THATCHER
1925–2013

SOURCE: From a speech to the National Union of Townswomen's Guilds Conference
DATE: 1965
FIELD: Politics

The wave of change in suffrage rights from the early part of the 20th century meant that by the 1960s political glass ceilings were being shattered all around the world. In 1966, Indira Gandhi became the first female prime minister of India; Shirley Chisholm became the first black woman to serve in the United States Congress in 1968; and Golda Meir became the first female prime minister of Israel in 1969. These women became beacons of female empowerment; for the first time, millions of young women were growing up in nations led by women.

At the height of the women's liberation movement, in 1974, Margaret Thatcher, a woman from a working-class background, became the leader of the UK's Conservative Party. These words opposite came from a speech nearly a decade earlier, when she was an MP, working her way up the political ladder. When she joined the cabinet in 1970 a journalist asked her if she ever hoped to be prime minister. "There will not be a woman prime minister in my lifetime," she replied, "the male population is too prejudiced."

In a 1978 interview, Thatcher famously said she wasn't a feminist, and when she did become prime minister in 1979, a premiership that lasted 11 years, she was quick to shed what little feminist rhetoric she might have been associated with. In 1982 on a children's TV show, when asked what she thought of women's lib, she said, "I'm not very keen on it." Despite her powerful position, Thatcher did little to advance women's rights and only promoted one woman to her cabinet.

The time has come for a new movement toward true equality for all women in America.

70

NATIONAL ORGANIZATION FOR WOMEN
Est. 1966

SOURCE: NOW Statement of Purpose
DATE: 1966
FIELD: Civil rights

In the postwar era, the strong feminist voices of the early 1900s had dwindled. Even with more and more women entering the workplace, the media enforced and celebrated the idea of the happy suburban housewife. However, the Civil Rights movement of the 1950s and 1960s spurred many women into action, as they fought for inclusion in equal rights legislation.

Title VII of the United States 1964 Civil Rights Act stated that it was unlawful for an employer to "fail to refuse to hire or to discharge any individual, or otherwise to discriminate against any individual with respect to his compensation, terms, conditions or privileges or employment, because of such individual's race, color, religion, sex, or national origin." The word "sex" was a late inclusion to the bill and provided legal protection for women facing discrimination in the workplace—something that up until that point had only existed in state law for those living in Hawaii and Wisconsin. Despite these changes, the Equal Employment Opportunity Commission (EEOC), which had been put in place to implement these new rights, voted in 1965 that sex segregation in job advertising was legal.

In 1966, at a national conference on women's rights, inspired by the activist organizations of the Civil Rights movement, Betty Friedan (see page 141) wrote the acronym NOW on a paper napkin. She gathered a small group of women in her hotel room and together they formed the National Organization for Women. Their goal was to take action to help women participate fully in American society, "in truly equal partnership with men."

Fashion, cosmetics, and feminine hygiene ads are aimed more at men than at women.

71

ELLEN WILLIS
1941-2006

SOURCE: *Ramparts*
DATE: 1969
FIELD: Cultural criticism

Among the issues that preoccupied the feminist movement of the late 1960s and early 1970s were abortion rights (see page 157), sex education, pornography, divorce rates, and domestic violence. Acknowledged in all of these was an embedded "sexism"—a social structure, reinforced by public policy, education, language, and the mass media that gave men power over women. Feminist criticism of advertising, in particular, was a prominent part of the movement by the 1970s. It focussed on brands such as Virginia Slims (cigarettes), whose female-targeted advertisements reeked of sexism. Among these critics was political and cultural commentator Ellen Willis, whose essay "Women and the Myth of Consumerism" offered a different perspective. Willis was the first pop-music critic of the *New Yorker*, and she wrote extensively until her death in 2006.

Radical feminism, of which Willis was a proponent, emerged in the USA in the 1960s. It more directly criticized and confronted male violence, domination, and sexual exploitation of women, than had earlier forms of feminism. Willis—who was one of the founding members of New York's Redstockings, a revolutionary women's liberation group—argued that all advertising turned women into sex objects. Her essay argued that, although society defined women as the primary consumers, wives actually had very little power over their husbands' money, and that advertising, while appearing to appeal to women, was actually targeting men by supporting the sexist status quo. She argued that women's subordination was being exploited by advertisers: "They encourage men to expect women to sport all the latest trappings of sexual slavery."

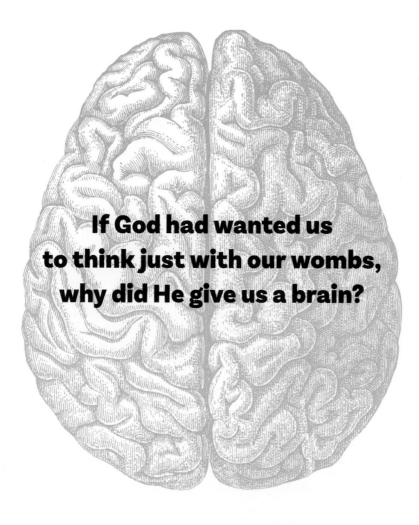

If God had wanted us
to think just with our wombs,
why did He give us a brain?

72

CLARE BOOTHE LUCE
1903–1987

SOURCE: From "A Doll's House 1970" in *Life* magazine
DATE: 1970
FIELDS: Journalism/diplomacy/politics

"Most of Clare Boothe Luce's life has been that of woman doing a man's job," *Life* magazine wrote in its October 16, 1970, issue. The introduction was followed by the writer and diplomat's one-act two-person play, a retelling of Henrik Ibsen's 1879 drama that questioned gender roles in 19th-century marriage (from which this much-quoted line comes) "rewritten in light of recent events." It was later retitled *Slam the Door Softly* after how the play ends, with the wife walking out on her husband, not wanting to be his "sleep-in, sleep-with body servant."

The "recent events" referred to are likely to have been the Women's Strike for Equality March, organized by the National Organization for Women (see page 145) and held on August 26, 1970, 50 years after the 19th Amendment granted women the right to vote. In New York alone, 50,000 feminists paraded down Fifth Avenue—they were joined by thousands of others in marches across the country. They had three goals: free abortion on demand, equal employment and educational opportunities, and the founding of round-the-clock childcare centers. The march took place in the same month that the House of Representatives passed the Equal Rights Amendment by a vote of 350–15.

Boothe Luce was a prolific playwright; she is best known for her 1936 satirical comedy *The Women*, in which she poked fun at her gender and wealthy social circle. *The Women* featured one of the largest all-female casts seen on Broadway and was a huge success, running for 657 performances and making its author $200,000, a considerable sum at the time.

I refuse to be
a female
impersonator.
I am a woman,
not a
- - - - - - -
castrate.

73

GERMAINE GREER
b. 1939

SOURCE: *The Female Eunuch*
DATE: 1970
FIELD: Social criticism

Seven years after Betty Friedan's *The Feminine Mystique* (see page 141), second-wave feminism was in full swing. The women's liberation movement of the 1960s had gathered momentum. Since the founding of more radical feminist groups—New York Radical Women and Redstockings among them—and the National Organization for Women in the United States, there had been internationally publicized walkouts and speak-outs by women on issues ranging from abortion rights to equal pay. In 1967, in the UK, the Abortion Act gave women the right to legal abortions on the National Health Service; in 1968, women of the Ford factory in Dagenham, Essex, UK, staged a strike for equal pay, almost shutting down Ford's UK operations completely.

At this time of burgeoning action and social change Australian-born academic Germaine Greer published her first book, *The Female Eunuch*. Translated into twelve languages, its first two print-runs quickly sold out, as women around the world feasted hungrily on Greer's humorous and abrasive celebration of the female body and female sexuality. A generation of women still consider Greer's seminal work life-changing. For all its (and Greer's) failures to live up to contemporary feminism's standards (its white, middle-class lens; its omission of abortion issues; her subsequent transphobic views; her suggestion that women drink their own menstrual blood), *The Female Eunuch* still resonates for many women today. Greer's impolite, unapologetic approach, in which she called for revolution not evolution, challenged women to become adventurers, and dared them to dream beyond a stop-gap job between education and motherhood.

Patriarchy,

reformed or unreformed,

is patriarchy still.

74

KATE MILLET
1934-2017

SOURCE: *Sexual Politics*
DATE: 1970
FIELD: Social criticism

Kate Millett was living a bohemian life in New York, attending meetings of
New York Radical Women, when *Sexual Politics* was published in 1970. She
was an artist with no intentions of becoming a leader of the second-wave
feminist movement in the USA, but the world had other plans. The book,
based on her Columbia University doctorate, sold 10,000 copies in the first
two weeks of release, and Millett was featured on the cover of *Time* magazine.
She became reluctant women's liberation royalty, all the while receiving
criticism for her fame and for her sexuality. *Sexual Politics* was a scathing attack
on the institutionalized power men have over women; it closely analyzed the
work of four male writers (Henry Miller, Norman Mailer, D. H. Lawrence,
and Jean Genet) to show how women are socialized to accept the patriarchy,
challenging the widely accepted notion that women are biologically and
innately subservient to men. It was a radical approach to feminist thinking.

Widely publicized texts like Millett's and Germaine Greer's (page 151)
introduced many young women to a new academic approach to feminism.
The first women's studies, black women's studies and lesbian studies courses
started to emerge in the 1970s (San Diego State University's women's studies
department became the first in the USA in 1970, for example). There was a
growing appetite for education, research, and analysis into women's issues,
providing an arena for feminists to discuss and develop their ideas—these
new departments were born from and became the "academic arm" of the
women's movement.

This is no simple reform. It really is a revolution.

75

GLORIA STEINEM
b. 1934

SOURCE: Address to the Women of America, NWPC organizing conference
DATE: 1971
FIELDS: Activism/journalism

After the United States Congress failed to pass the Equal Rights Amendment in 1970, which would have enshrined equal rights into the US Constitution, making it illegal to deny or abridge rights based on sex, a group of women formed the National Women's Political Caucus (NWPC). They believed that the economic and social equity they sought for all women could be best realized through equal representation among the country's decision-makers: the politicians. At the group's founding conference in July 1971, they called for action against "sexism, racism, institutional violence, and poverty." They pledged to train up female candidates for public office, encourage women to register to vote, and put women's issues at the forefront of election campaigns.

Gloria Steinem, one of feminism's most respected and outspoken voices of the late 20th century, was one of the NWPC's founding members. In her "Address to the Women of America" at the convention, she spoke about how gender and race, the "easy, visible differences," had been used to organize humans into inferior and superior groups. She envisioned a humanist society in which "there will be no roles other than those chosen or those earned." Steinem's career as a journalist sat alongside her activism. She co-founded Voters for Choice and the Coalition of Labor Union Women and was responsible for starting *Ms.* magazine in 1971—at that point the only national publication edited and controlled by women. Steinem, who is now in her eighties, is still an extremely active part of the women's movement; she famously delivered a speech at the 2017 Women March on Washington, in which she declared: "We will not be quiet. We will not be controlled."

If men could get pregnant, abortion would be a sacrament.

76

FLORYNCE KENNEDY
1916–2001

SOURCE: *Off Our Backs*
DATE: ca. 1971
FIELDS: Activism/abortion rights

Known to everyone as "Flo," Florynce Kennedy was one of the first black women to graduate from New York's Columbia Law School. She opened her own law firm, but also used her brains, intellectual wit, and charisma as a political activist. She set up the Media Workshop, an organization that aimed to fight racism in the press and advertising, and she founded the Feminist Party in 1971. She lectured widely with Gloria Steinem (see page 155), which is when the two women were thought to have overheard a Boston taxi driver say the words opposite, words they both repeated often.

State laws banned and restricted abortions in the late 1800s. By the 1950s and '60s, there were as many as 1.2 million illegal abortions each year. In the USA, the radical feminist group Redstockings, appalled at the omission of female speakers at legislative hearings on abortion law, organized the 1969 Abortion Speak Out, and tried to shift the public conversation from rape and incest to a woman's right to choose. Together with a feminist legal team, Flo Kennedy gathered personal testimony from women who had experienced illegal abortions and presented it in open deposition as part of a class-action lawsuit targeting New York's antiabortion law. Four years later, the historic decision of the Supreme Court in Roe v. Wade (1973) made it legal to have an abortion in all states. It ruled that Americans' right to privacy included a woman's right to decide whether to have children, without interference from the state. However, despite the court's decisiveness, antiabortion activists hit back, trying to restrict funding, protesting outside clinics, and in many cases attacking abortion practitioners. The struggle for abortion rights in America continues to this day.

Men have been the
conquerors since ancient
days, and the story
of mankind has been
a bloody one.

AÐALHEIÐUR BJARNFREÐSDÓTTIR
1921–1994

SOURCE: Rally speech on "Women's Day Off"
DATE: 1975
FIELDS: Trade unionism/politics

On October 24, 1975, something unusual happened in Iceland. An estimated 90 percent of the country's women went on strike. They didn't cook, or clean, or go to their jobs. Instead, 25,000 of them gathered in Reykjavik to be part of an unprecedented rally (the country's population was only 220,000), organized in the wake of the United Nations (UN) declaring 1975 International Women's Year (International Women's Day was adopted by the UN that year and has been celebrated internationally on March 8 ever since). An Icelandic committee of women's organizations arranged the event to remind society of the essential and undervalued role women played in it. They called it the Women's Day Off. Many of the country's institutions had to shut down for the day, their workforces depleted; fathers had to take their children to work.

Aðalheiður Bjarnfreðsdóttir, a mother and trade union leader, representing some of the country's lowest-paid women, was one of the rally's main speakers, alongside two MPs, a housewife, a female worker, and a representative of the women's movement. Aðalheiður was last to speak and the words opposite captured the spirit of that day. It was time for change, and that change was only going to come through cooperation. "Nothing is farther from our intentions than to suppress the men," she said. "We want equality: nothing more or less." Aðalheiður went on to become a congress member in Iceland's parliament.

Five years after the Women's Day Off, Vigdís Finnbogadóttir, a divorced single mother, won Iceland's presidency, making her Europe's first female president and the first woman in the world to be democratically elected as a head of state.

I have a brain
and a uterus, and
I use both.

78

PATRICIA SCHROEDER
b. 1940

SOURCE: *People* magazine
DATE: 1977
FIELD: Politics

When Patricia Schroeder, the 32-year-old newly elected congresswoman from Colorado, was finding her feet in Washington, DC, in 1972, she was approached by one of her male colleagues. "How can you be the mother of two small children and a member of Congress at the same time," he asked her. The quote opposite was her reply. Schroeder's election victory had been a shock even to her, but her anti-Vietnam War and stance on women's issues had seen the people of her home district send their first woman to the House of Representatives. Schroeder once described her workplace as "an over-aged frat house." Like many women in the 1970s embarking on careers in male-dominated industries, when the term "sexual harassment" didn't exist, she faced the "boys' club" sexism in an institution where there were just fourteen congresswomen, compared to 421 men.

Schroeder's can-do attitude meant she plowed on, raising her children (she was known to carry diapers in her bag on the House floor) and pursuing her political goals, regardless of her own doubts, the media attention, and the criticism she received from her peers. She became a stalwart of Capitol Hill, serving 12 terms—24 years in office—before deciding to step down. She worked hard to make changes in the military—Cold War spending, arms control, and women's roles in particular—and as a vocal feminist and pro-choice advocate, she dedicated her career to improving women's healthcare and equality in the workplace, including changing the laws around maternity leave and female genital mutilation.

The connections between and among women are the most feared, the most problematic, and the most potentially transforming force on the planet.

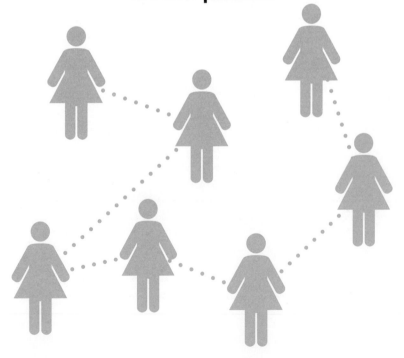

79

ADRIENNE RICH
1929–2012

SOURCE: *On Lies, Secrets, and Silence*
DATE: 1979
FIELDS: Feminist writing/poetry

The 1970s saw a growing rift between heterosexual feminism and lesbian feminism. The predominantly white, heteronormative, middle-class movement was failing to speak to the many women who did not fall under its banner. In a 1981 publication by a group of British feminists entitled "Love Your Enemy: The Debate Between Heterosexual Feminism and Political Lesbianism," it said that "all feminists can and should be lesbians." The booklet caused outrage among the feminist community. The acts of these revolutionary feminists, and others like them, who were keen to distance themselves from the violence and oppression they associated with heterosexuality, had a knock-on effect on the wider movement. They drew much criticism for causing feminism in general to be depicted in the media as the purview of man-hating "angry lesbians"—an image that has deterred many women from identifying themselves as feminists.

Adrienne Rich, a renowned American poet and essayist, who was herself a lesbian, wrote widely about the gay experience in a 1980 essay *Compulsory Heterosexuality and Lesbian Existence*. She was one of a group of intellectuals committed to challenging stereotypes and breaking down the taboos surrounding sexuality. She wanted to reinforce what she saw as the hugely important political and personal bonds between women, and to encourage women to reorient their lives around each other, rather than around men. She saw the social benefits of female companionship and support prevalent in some lesbian communities that were not necessarily available to heterosexual women.

Pornography incarnates male supremacy.

It is the DNA of male dominance.

80

ANDREA DWORKIN
1946-2005

SOURCE: *Pornography: Men Possessing Women*
DATE: 1981
FIELD: Pornography activism

When Andrea Dworkin died in 2005, aged just 58, it was the end of one of radical feminism's most consistent and assiduous voices. For nearly 40 years, the American activist campaigned tirelessly against misogyny, pornography, and the abuse of women. She wrote widely on the subject, particularly in *Pornography: Men Possessing Women*, in which she analyzed the form, and argued that its consumption encouraged men to eroticize the exploitation, domination, and degradation of women.

In the early 1980s Dworkin, together with legal scholar Catharine MacKinnon, became famous after drafting an ordinance for Minneapolis City Council, Minnesota, that recognized pornography as sex discrimination and a violation of women's civil rights. The legislation was intended to allow people to sue pornographers for damages by showing that they had suffered harm from its making or use. Women from all over the country who had worked in the porn industry gave evidence. The law was passed, but it was later overturned in federal court. Rather than banning or censoring porn, encouraging women to bring lawsuits was a feminist approach that brought Dworkin much notoriety and lead to her and MacKinnon testifying for the Meese Commission in 1986 (a right-wing attempt, under the Reagan administration, to prove the harmful effects that pornography had on the public). Yet feminists were divided; many feared that a crackdown on violent or degrading pornography would lead to censorship of other sexually explicit materials. To the liberal left, Dworkin became something of a hate figure, and her own experiences of rape and domestic violence, as well as her body image, were used to mock and discredit her in the media.

"Woman" was the test,
but not every woman
seemed to qualify.

81

ANGELA DAVIS
b. 1944

SOURCE: Women, Race, and Class
DATE: 1981
FIELDS: Racial equality/activism

Since the earliest days of slavery, black women have faced intersectional discrimination—the manifold oppressions of gender, race, and class, in a world where poverty disproportionately affects nonwhite communities—unmatched by their white counterparts. It was what led Sojourner Truth to ask, "And ain't I a woman?" in 1851 (see page 67) and also what led many women of color to be more critical of mainstream feminism from the 1960s onward.

It was also what feminist and activist Angela Davis wrote about in her groundbreaking book, *Women, Race, and Class*, which traced the feminist movement and the actions of predominantly white, middle-class women to achieve suffrage. Davis laid out how the white women's movement did not fully understand or appreciate the needs of the working-class black community, exploring the profoundly different experiences of black and white women when it came to reproductive rights, working conditions, and sexual assault and rape. Despite white radical feminists in the 1970s being committed to racial equality, the movement was not attractive to black women, who were politically engaged in black nationalism. Davis argued that the movement was not radical enough; it failed to address economic inequality.

Angela Davis was well known for her Communist Party and Black Panther affiliations. In 2017, she was an honorary co-chair of the Women's March on Washington (see page 205), at which she said, "This is a women's march [that] represents [...] an inclusive and intersectional feminism that calls upon all of us to join the resistance to racism, to Islamophobia, to anti-Semitism, to misogyny, to capitalist exploitation."

Womanist is to feminist
as purple to lavender.

82

ALICE WALKER
b. 1944

SOURCE: *In Search of Our Mother's Gardens: Womanist Prose*
DATE: 1983
FIELDS: Womanism/literature

The extreme racism and sexism faced by women of color in the 1960s led to criticism of mainstream feminism (see page 167), as well as the founding in the 1970s of organizations committed to fighting it, such as the National Black Feminist Organization and the Combahee River Collective. It was also what led author and activist Alice Walker to coin and define the term "womanism" in 1983. Walker had already brought black women's lives to the fore in her novels, most famously in *The Color Purple*, for which she won the Pulitzer Prize for Fiction (the first African-American woman to do so). With womanism, she sought to achieve the same prominence for black feminism. She defined a womanist as a black feminist or feminist of color, who loves other women (both sexually and non-sexually), who appreciates and prefers women's culture, "emotional flexibility," and strength.

This deeper, more potent "purple" feminism (to mainstream feminism's "lavender") acknowledged the needs and struggles of black women and their communities. Unlike mainstream feminism, which had largely been focused on the liberation and empowerment of women alone, making it somewhat of a separatist movement, womanism recognized the integral role black men and black children played in the lives of black women. It spoke to the unique oppressions and problems they faced as a result, as well as the different relationship black women have to men, compared to white women. Womanists wanted equality and liberation not just for women but for all African Americans. Walker's womanism was influential in redefining feminism and broadening the mainstream movement to be more inclusive of women of color.

I write for those women who do not speak [...] because they, we, are so terrified, because we are taught to respect fear more than ourselves.

83

AUDRE LORDE
1934–1992

SOURCE: "My Words Will Be There," first published in *Black Women Writers (1950–1980): A Critical Evaluation*
DATE: 1983
FIELDS: Poetry/feminist theory

Audre Lorde often introduced herself as a "Black Lesbian Feminist Poet Mother"—her self-styled title part of the confrontational creativity for which she became well known. She broached intersectional discrimination and the marginalization of the various social groups she bridged, while refusing to be categorized. Her poetry dealt with love, lesbianism, family relationships, and later civil rights and sex discrimination, and she came under fire from conservatives, who criticized the graphic and sexual nature of her radical approach. Lorde was one of the first high-profile black feminists to challenge heteronormative points of view and encourage other women to reclaim eroticism for their own pleasure. Despite the racist, sexist, and homophobic criticism she received, Lorde's poetry remained unapologetic and passionate to the last. She refused to cower in fear; she refused to be silenced.

Lorde's first poem was published in *Seventeen* magazine when she was just 15. She went on to publish a number of successful poetry volumes, including *The Black Unicorn* (1978). In 1980 she released a highly acclaimed personal account, *The Cancer Journals*, detailing her battle with breast cancer. She chose not to wear a prosthesis after undergoing a mastectomy because she felt that by visibly expressing her experience, it would help other women to overcome the silence and stigma attached to the procedure. She died from the disease in 1992. In the essay this quotation comes from, she asked herself what she had to share with the younger generation of writers. "I can tell them not to be afraid to feel and not to be afraid to write about it," she said. "Even if you are afraid, do it anyway."

There will be no mass-based feminist movement as long as feminist ideas are understood only by a well-educated few.

84

BELL HOOKS
b. 1952

SOURCE: *Feminist Theory: From Margin to Center*
DATE: 1984
FIELDS: Feminist theory/education

When Gloria Jean Watkins chose a pen name for her feminist and cultural writings, she settled on "bell hooks," her maternal great-grandmother's name, a woman who was known to speak her mind. She chose the lower-case presentation to emphasize her work's importance over her own importance. With over thirty publications under this name, covering personal memoir, cultural criticism, and poetry, she has continued to do just that, opening up the feminist debate to include marginalized groups, women of color, and less-educated women in particular.

One such book included the essay "Educating Women: A Feminist Agenda," in which she expressed the contemporary feminist movement's failure to address the connection between sexual exploitation and the level of education of its victims. She argued that the ability to read and write, something not all women possessed, was a vital component of change. It enables women to convey and share ideas and information, think for themselves, and imagine ways to create change. She also recognized that writing was the most accessible and affordable form of mass communication—in the 1980s feminists still largely distributed their ideas this way, meaning illiterate women were unable to easily learn about their cause. This, she believed, had led to a conflict between bourgeois theorists, disconnected from reality, and anti-theoretical, anti-intellectual feminists, who were often uneducated black women. She advocated for women's studies courses to be held at local community centers, making them available to the less privileged, and encouraged women to both strive for more education and intellectual understanding, and help each other to find ways to think analytically and systematically about society.

85

MARGARET ATWOOD
b. 1939

SOURCE: *The Handmaid's Tale*
DATE: 1985
FIELD: Literature

When Canadian author Margaret Atwood imagined the fictional world of *The Handmaid's Tale* in 1984, she was living in West Berlin, encircled by the Berlin Wall. She envisioned a dystopian world order in which the United States was no more and the Republic of Gilead stood in its place. Atwood's theocratic patriarchy, where infertility is rife, saw fertile women—handmaids—forced to perform their godly duty by providing children for the highest social class and their older, infertile wives.

It is Atwood's protagonist, a handmaid the reader knows as Offred, who discovers the scrawled message (opposite) in mock Latin scratched in the wardrobe of her room by her predecessor, a handmaid who had committed suicide. The message is later roughly translated in the book as, "Don't let the bastards grind you down." And in the years since the novel's publication, the phrase has becoming something of a rallying cry for feminists, with some women even choosing to have it tattooed on their bodies.

The novel was released at the height of a backlash against feminism in the United States. In 1982, the Equal Rights Amendment had reached its deadline and failed to pass; anti-feminist campaigner Phyllis Schlafly had galvanized the "family values" movement; and the New Christian Right campaigned against women's right to abortion. *The Handmaid's Tale* can be seen as a response to that—Atwood created an alien and terrifying world that resonated with real life and many people's fears about the future. This same sentiment was echoed in 2017, when pro-choice campaigners dressed in handmaid costumes to protest the passing of Texas state laws that would restrict abortion rights.

It's true what they say about women:
Women are insatiable.
We are greedy.

86

NAOMI WOLF
b. 1962

SOURCE: *The Beauty Myth*
DATE: 1990
FIELDS: Beauty standards/media

Where the second-wave feminists of the 1960s and 1970s had Betty Friedan's *The Feminine Mystique* (see page 141) and Germaine Greer's *The Female Eunuch* (see page 151), young women in the 1990s had Naomi Wolf's international bestseller, *The Beauty Myth*. These women, many of whom had grown up with second-wave feminist mothers, were part of an emerging "third wave" of feminism. This movement grew out of the decades of women's studies university programs, feminist media outlets, and long-standing feminist organizations, and it was awake to the sexist, racist, and classist barriers that still presented themselves. It critiqued society's depiction, treatment, and expectation of women through media and advertising that created the beauty myth, the "last, best belief system that keeps male dominance intact."

Wolf's book, while reiterating much of what women had been writing about for decades, repackaged it for a new generation. Although Western women had more rights than ever before, it was also the era of the supermodel and an eating disorder epidemic; the era of anti-aging advertisements; and the growth of surgical cosmetic procedures. The way women looked seemed to be valued by society more than it ever had. *The Beauty Myth* talked about the cultural conspiracy of capitalism, in which women are constantly made to feel inadequate, so they will buy more, and how this myth alone is enough to prevent equality being realized. Women who are not controlled by the patriarchy, and who love their bodies and their femaleness, champion the rights of other women and ask for "more love, more sex, more money, more commitment to children, more food, more care."

Human rights are women's rights and women's rights are human rights.

87

HILLARY CLINTON
b. 1947

SOURCE: From a speech at the United Nations Fourth World
Conference on Women
DATE: 1995
FIELD: Politics

In September 1995, 47,000 feminist activists from across the world came
together in Beijing, China, for the United Nations World Conference on
Women. It was thought to be the largest gathering of its kind in history.
Leading the US delegation was first lady Hillary Clinton, who delivered one
of the event's most memorable speeches, in which she said, "If there is one
message that echoes forth from this conference, let it be that human rights are
women's rights and women's rights are human rights, once and for all." Her
words came in the wake of the 1989 Tiananmen Square massacre, in which
several hundred civilian protestors were shot dead by the Chinese army, and
the April 1995 arrest of Nobel Peace Prize nominee Wei Jingsheng, a pro-
democracy Chinese dissident. Clinton addressed these human rights violations
when she said, "Let us not forget that among those rights are the right to speak
freely, and the right to be heard."

While Clinton's words have been repeated often since, her presence at the
conference itself was considered controversial. American politicians and
diplomats felt strongly that the first lady should not be criticizing a foreign
government, especially as a guest in China, and that while women's rights were
important, Clinton's speaking about them elevated the issue above other world
events. Yet Clinton felt personally compelled to be there, whether she was sent
officially or not. As a senator herself, she went on to champion a number of
women's causes, such as advocating childcare funding, access to emergency
contraception, and equal pay. In 2016, she became the first woman in the
USA to earn a major party's nomination for president.

The time
has come to
leave the old ways
of suffering
behind.

88

WARIS DIRIE
b. 1965

SOURCE: *Desert Flower*
DATE: 1997
FIELD: Female genital mutilation

Waris Dirie was 5 years old when she was subjected to female genital mutilation
(FGM) in Somalia. The barbaric procedure, which causes many girls to die
from blood loss or infection, can involve the removal of the clitoral hood or
the excision of the entire external genitalia. The vaginal opening is then sewn
up, leaving only a small hole for urine and menstrual blood. Women have
lasting complications, including painful sex and problems urinating, and may
even die during childbirth. The procedure is done in the belief girls will grow
up "clean," ensuring their virginity remains intact for marriage.

Dirie survived, but after learning of an impending marriage to a man in his
sixties (she was 13), the headstrong teenager fled, running through the desert
for days to relatives in Mogadishu. Eventually she arrived in London, where at
18 she was discovered by a fashion photographer and began what would become
a very successful career as a model. In 1997, haunted by the knowledge that this
was still happening to 8,000 girls every day, according to the World Health
Organization, she told her story to the world, through interviews, her
biography *Desert Flower*, and as a UN Goodwill Ambassador.

In 2002 Dirie set up the Desert Flower Foundation to raise awareness of
female genital mutilation, carry out prevention work, and help and guide FGM
victims to regain their confidence and improve their quality of life. In the years
since, there have been some significant changes in international human rights
law and national laws banning FGM. However, anti-FGM activists believe
there is still much work to do. In the UK, for example, where FGM has been a
criminal offense since 1985, prosecutions are scarce.

Consciousness is everything. Even now, acknowledging inequality begs one to do something about it.

89

JENNIFER BAUMGARDNER / AMY RICHARDS
b. 1970 / b. 1971

SOURCE: Manifesta: Young Women, Feminism and the Future
DATE: 2000
FIELD: Third-wave feminism

In the 1990s a new kind of female self-empowerment emerged. Third-wave feminism saw young women question, reclaim, and subvert existing ideas about gender and sexism. A "girlie culture" developed that embraced personal experience, femininity, and sexual self-esteem. It was widely criticized by second-wavers, who saw the new generation's concerns as trivial and out of line with the equality they had fought for. The focus of much third-wave feminist writing was lived experience—struggles with eating disorders, body image, sexual assault, and racial difference, for example. And the movement brought with it a new take on sexist, derogatory language, with women proudly declaring themselves "bitches" or "sluts." It was the age of Riot Grrrl bands (an activism that fused feminist politics with punk rock), pop culture, female icons like Madonna, and new powerful, sexually defiant television characters in shows like *Buffy the Vampire Slayer* and *Sex and the City*.

In *Manifesta*, New York journalists Jennifer Baumgardner and Amy Richards sought to revive the feminist cause by highlighting these intergenerational issues, inspiring younger readers and hoping to unite American women around a 21st-century feminism (albeit largely from a liberal, white, middle-class perspective). They set out a thirteen-point agenda that included safeguarding reproductive rights, raising awareness of feminist revolutionary history, and supporting lesbian and bisexual women, female participation in the military, flexible working, and the passing of the Equal Rights Amendment. They also acknowledged that, "although feminists may have disparate values, we share the same goal of equality."

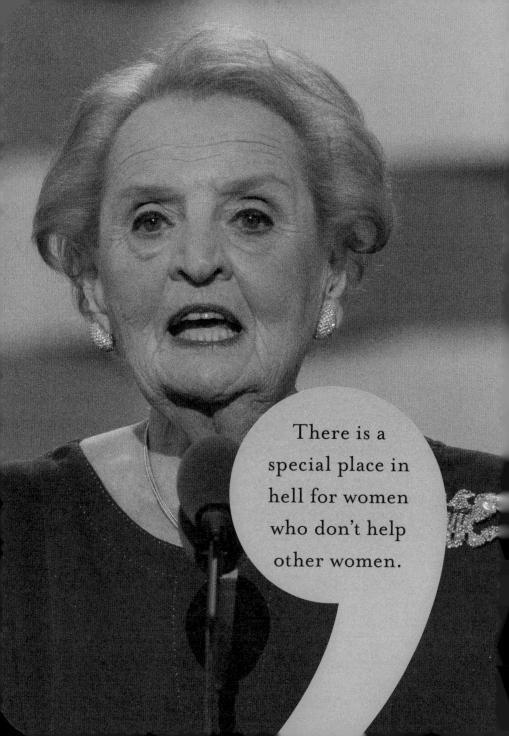

There is a special place in hell for women who don't help other women.

90

MADELEINE ALBRIGHT
b. 1937

SOURCE: From a speech given at a WNBA luncheon
DATES: 2006
FIELD: Politics

When Madeleine Albright was made the first female American Secretary of State in 1997, she became the highest-ranking woman in the history of US politics at that time. She decided that women's issues had to be central to American foreign policy because she believed that societies are better off when women are politically and economically empowered. Albright had previously worked as the country's permanent representative to the United Nations, where she set up a caucus of other female representatives to lobby in support of women's issues.

This quote has become something of a trademark for Albright, and it is regularly repeated by her and others. It even found its way onto Starbucks coffee cups. In one 2010 interview, Albright contextualized the statement, saying that it was very important for women to help each other, because it was hard to be the only woman in the room—something she was very familiar with. "I think there has to be the sense that once you have climbed the ladder of success you don't push it away from the building," she said. "You are only strengthened if there are more women." In 2016 the same quotation caused some controversy when Albright used it to introduce Democratic presidential candidate Hillary Clinton at a campaign event. Many women took offense at the insinuation that they should vote for Hillary purely because of her gender.

Albright has helped pull many women up the ladder behind her, most notably through the work of the Albright Institute at her alma mater Wellesley College, and through her work as chair of the National Democratic Institute, working to support female political candidates.

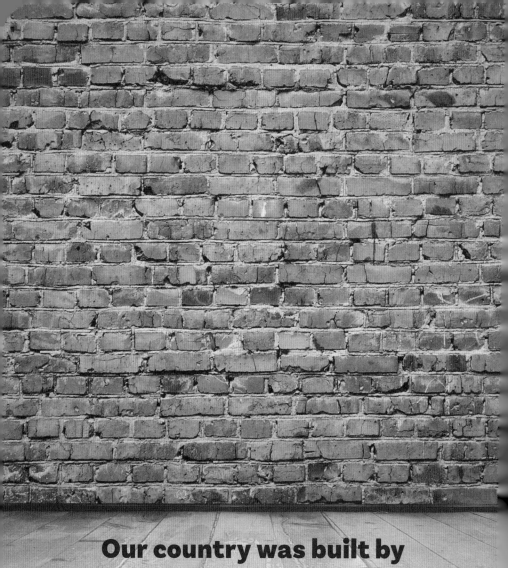

Our country was built by strong women, and we will continue to break down walls and defy stereotypes.

91

NANCY PELOSI
b. 1940

SOURCE: *Glamour*
DATE: 2007
FIELD: Politics

The late 20th and early 21st century saw women breaking down the walls and defying the stereotypes American politician Nancy Pelosi spoke about—from tennis-player Billie Jean King demanding equal prize money at the US Open in 1973 and Sandra Day O'Connor's appointment to the Supreme Court in 1981 to Dame Margaret Anstee's appointment as Under-Secretary-General at the UN in 1987. And in 2007, when Pelosi became the 52nd Speaker of the House of Representatives, she broke down a wall of her own. "Women are leaders everywhere you look," she said, "from the CEO who runs a Fortune 500 company to the housewife who raises her children and heads her household." Pelosi has remained in politics as the House Democratic leader since and continues to be included on the Forbes' "most powerful women" list. Despite facing sexism, ageism, and her own party's derision, she has been called the "strongest and most effective speaker of modern times."

Over a decade since Pelosi broke that specific glass ceiling, there are still plenty of important roles women have yet to fill, especially in the United States, where there has still not been a female president or vice-president, chief justice of the Supreme Court, director of the FBI or CIA, or Secretary of Defense, Treasury, or Veterans Affairs. Elsewhere, there has still not been a woman UN Secretary-General, British Chancellor of the Exchequer, leader of the UK's Labour Party, or Governor of the Bank of England. Most of the world's countries have never had a female head of government or state.

If you're going
to change
things,

you have to
be with the
people who
hold the levers.

92

RUTH BADER GINSBURG
b. 1933

SOURCE: *The New York Times*
DATE: 2009
FIELD: Judiciary

In 1950, for the first time, 14 women joined a class of 520 men to take their seats at Harvard Law School. Each month there was a single class, known as Ladies Day, when the women students were invited to speak. Ruth Bader Ginsburg joined Harvard Law School 6 years later, where she was one of only nine women students. She would go on to graduate from Columbia Law School joint first in her class. After founding the *Women's Rights Law Reporter*, the first American law journal with a singular focus on women's rights, she went one better, setting up the Women's Rights Project at the American Civil Liberties Union (a nonprofit organization that defends the constitutional rights of citizens through lobbying and litigation) to argue landmark gender equality cases.

This quotation comes from an interview in which Ginsburg was asked why she chose to work with the ACLU, in coalition with men, rather than through a women's organization. "I always thought that there was nothing an antifeminist would want more than to have women only in women's organizations, in their own little corner," she said. Ginsburg fought discrimination in the courts strategically, often selecting male plaintiffs to illustrate how unequal laws were bad for everyone. In the years since, she has spoken widely and often about equality, with a specific focus on the importance of men and women sharing the responsibilities of housework and childcare. In 1993 she became the second woman to be appointed Associate Justice of the Supreme Court in the United States.

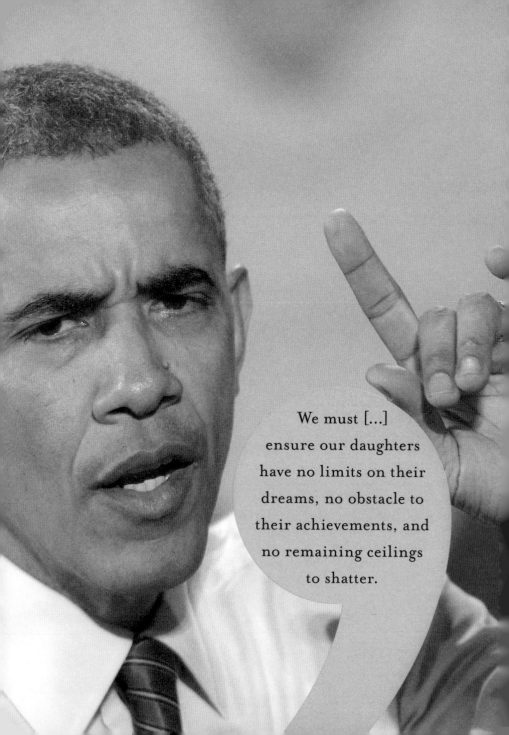

We must [...] ensure our daughters have no limits on their dreams, no obstacle to their achievements, and no remaining ceilings to shatter.

93

BARACK OBAMA
b.1961

SOURCE: In a Presidential Proclamation ahead of the centenary of
International Women's Day
DATE: 2011
FIELD: Politics

"I may be a little grayer than I was 8 years ago," said President Barack Obama to
the crowd of thousands gathered in Washington, DC, at the first White House
Summit on the United State of Women in 2016, "but this is what a feminist
looks like. Of course, in my household, there's no choice." Obama's historic
election to the highest political office in the United States in 2008, as the
country's first African-American president, was also significant for another
reason—he was the first openly feminist president too.

For a country that has yet to see a woman holding the highest position in
political office, it was consoling to see Obama focus efforts on changes to
improve the lives of women and girls. The first piece of legislation he signed
into law was the Lilly Ledbetter Fair Pay Act. Named after an Alabama woman
who fought a 10-year-long pay discrimination case against her employer, the
new law expanded workers' rights to sue for pay discrimination, relaxing the
statute of limitations. He also defended a woman's right to choose and in the
final days of his administration introduced regulations that prevented states
from withholding federal funds from Planned Parenthood affiliates and other
clinics that provided abortions. The household that Obama spoke about in
2016 included his two teenage daughters and first lady Michelle Obama, whose
own feminist work included leading Let Girls Learn, an international initiative
to help adolescent girls get the education they deserve. At the same summit,
in conversation with Oprah Winfrey, Michelle Obama urged men to "be
better at everything."

In the future, there will be no female leaders. There will just be leaders.

94

SHERYL SANDBERG
b. 1969

SOURCE: *Lean In: Women, Work, and the Will to Lead*
DATE: 2013
FIELDS: Business/women in the workplace

What started as a speech at the 2010 TED Conference became a global catchphrase and a movement, galvanizing women to "lean in" at work and for men to take an equal responsibility for childcare. Sheryl Sandberg, the COO of Facebook, published *Lean In: Women, Work, and the Will to Lead* a couple of years after gracing the TEDWomen stage and talking about the lack of progress being made in corporations, regarding gender parity in the boardroom and the adversity women face in the workplace. While the book was criticized for focusing heavily on the lives of privileged, educated women in corporate jobs, rather than low-earners and single mothers, it offered practical advice as to how women could negotiate their salary, speak up in meetings, and set boundaries to help balance their job with life outside of work.

One of the direct impacts of the book was the establishment of Leanin.org, a nonprofit organization that had the mission statement "to empower women to achieve their ambitions" through education, raising public awareness, and through Lean In Circles—small peer groups that meet regularly to help bring about these changes. As of 2018, there were 36,000 circles around the world. A 2017 study, conducted by the organization, found that there was still a long way to go before Sandberg's goal of 50 percent of companies being run by women was realized. Despite the fact women earned 57 percent of college degrees in the United States, they found only one in five top-level executives was a woman, and only one in 30 was a woman of color. Of the Fortune 500 CEO jobs, only 5 percent were filled by women.

We call upon our sisters around the world to be brave—to embrace the strength within themselves and realize their full potential.

95

MALALA YOUSAFZAI
b. 1997

SOURCE: Speech at the United Nations
DATE: 2013
FIELDS: Equal rights/education

In the mid-1800s, when women were beginning to be admitted into universities, it would have been hard to imagine a time when there were more women than men pursuing higher education. Yet that time is now, in the 21st century. However, this positive global trend masks a deep-rooted continuing bias against women in education—from textbooks and teachers to participation. Illiteracy disproportionately affects women around the world, with girls far more likely never to enter primary school than boys. In some countries, families simply cannot afford to keep their children in school; elsewhere, lack of feminine hygiene products and education around menstruation prevent girls from regular school attendance.

In the Swat Valley, Pakistan, in 2008, it was the edict of Taliban militants that prevented girls from taking their rightful place in the classroom. Malala Yousafzai was one of those girls. At just 12 years old she started blogging for the BBC about her experience living under the oppressive regime and the ban it imposed on girls in schools. After the Taliban were forced to retreat in 2011, Yousafzai's school finally reopened, but her journalism and public campaigning for girls' education made her a target for Taliban fighters. And on October 9, 2012, a masked gunman boarded her school bus, asked for her by name and shot her in the head, neck, and shoulder. Yousafzai was transported to the UK for treatment and survived. Since recovering from the ordeal, Yousafzai has become an international advocate and fundraiser for girls' education and equality. This quote comes from the speech she gave to the UN on her sixteenth birthday.

All of us, women and men, must do better.

96

CHIMAMANDA NGOZI ADICHIE
b. 1977

SOURCE: *We Should All Be Feminists*
DATE: 2014
FIELD: Equality

In 2012, award-winning Nigerian author Chimamanda Ngozi Adichie delivered a talk at TEDxEuston entitled "We Should All Be Feminists." Viewed millions of times online in the years since, Adichie's talk explored her own feminism and its place in Nigerian culture, the awkward and difficult conversations people try to avoid about gender, and the wider implications of gender roles around the world, where women are oppressed and excluded, while men are expected to be dominant models of hyper-masculinity. She argued that if we want a more just, more equal world, we need to raise our children differently. Two years later an adaptation of the essay was published as a book, catapulting Adichie from Baltimore-based novelist to internationally acclaimed feminist. While the author has spoken publicly about some negative reactions she has received from fans of her previous books to her feminist stance, she has not been deterred, speaking widely on the topic and publishing a second book in which she offered a friend advice on how to raise her daughter to be a feminist.

In 2015, the Swedish Women's Lobby distributed a free copy of the book to every 16-year-old in Sweden in the hope that teachers would integrate it into their curriculum and that it would open up a conversation about gender and gender roles among young people. Adichie's words have also become part of popular culture, with Beyoncé sampling part of the TEDx talk in a song in 2013 and fashion house Dior collaborating with the author to create T-shirts with the talk's title emblazoned across them in 2016.

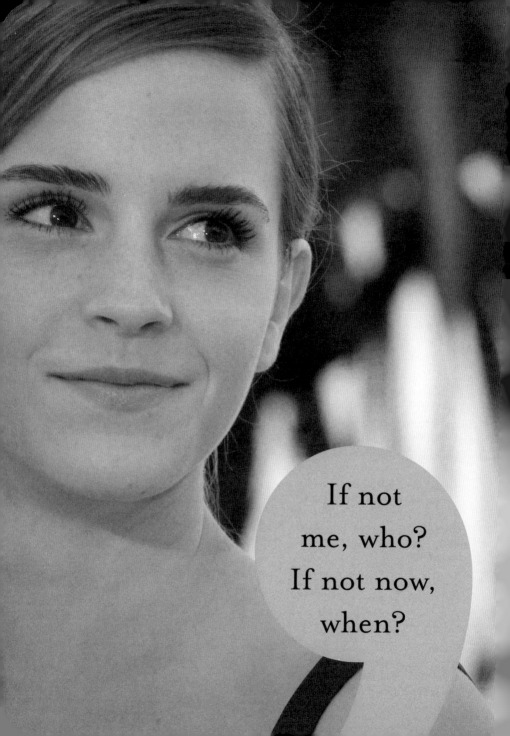

If not me, who? If not now, when?

97

EMMA WATSON
b. 1990

SOURCE: From a speech at the United Nations Headquarters, New York
DATE: 2014
FIELD: Equality

When Emma Watson took to the podium at the United Nations Headquarters in New York, she was probably still best known for playing Hermione Granger in the internationally successful Harry Potter film franchise. She had recently been appointed a goodwill ambassador for UN Women, the United Nations entity that is dedicated to gender equality and empowering women. She was hosting the launch of "HeForShe," a new campaign to encourage women and men to stand together in solidarity for a gender-equal world.

Watson's speech garnered lots of public attention. In it she talked of her own journey as a feminist and spoke about not only how gender inequality was still prevalent in much of the world for women but also how it negatively impacted men. She said that both men and women should be free to be sensitive and to be strong, and that we should perceive gender on a spectrum rather than as two opposing ideals, making the world an equal and better place for all. She ended her speech with a call to action, asking the "inadvertent feminists" of the world, those who believe in equality, to pledge to make a change. "I am inviting you to step forward," she said, "to be seen to speak up, to be the 'he' for 'she.' And to ask yourself, if not me, who? If not now, when?"

Within three days of the speech 100,000 men from all over the world had pledged their support. At the time of writing, there are 1.7 million pledges. In 2015, HeForShe launched the Impact 10x10x10 initiative that convened ten heads of state, global CEOs and university presidents to help fast-track gender inequality in politics, boardrooms, and classrooms.

Women are silenced by both the invisibility and the acceptability of the problem.

98

LAURA BATES
b. 1986

SOURCE: *Everyday Sexism*
DATE: 2014
FIELD: Sexism

Many women around the world now have the right to attend school, get a job, vote, run for office, marry whom they choose, access contraception, take paid maternity leave, and have an abortion. To some, it might seem that the fight is over, that parity has been achieved. Yet as most women know, even in countries with these rights, they are severely underrepresented in positions of power, from governments and judiciaries to academia and the arts. The gender pay gap still exists, and women suffer disproportionately from sexual discrimination in the workplace, domestic violence and murder, sexual assault, and rape. And then there are the "little things," the common occurrences of sexism that feminist writer Laura Bates described as "reams of tiny pinpricks" that make up life as a woman. In 2012, she set up the Everyday Sexism Project to provide women with a platform to talk about these "pinpricks."

The project's simple website allowed women to share their sexist experiences, and it built up a shocking picture of the barrage of abuse, harassment, and discrimination women deal with on a daily basis. Within 18 months of the project starting, it had expanded with companion sites in 18 other countries, and nearly a year after its launch there were 50,000 entries. The comments posted on the site were used by British parliamentarians to push for a change in sex and relationships education in schools, and Bates also used women's stories to help the London Transport Police tackle unwanted sexual behavior on the city's public transport network.

I'm going to keep
saying loud and clear
"I'm a feminist" until
it is met with a shrug.

99

JUSTIN TRUDEAU
b. 1971

SOURCE: UN Women "Step it Up" summit, New York
DATE: 2016
FIELD: Politics

In 2015, Justin Trudeau made Canadian history when he announced a cabinet that had a 50:50 gender split: the nation's first. "It's important to be here before you today to present to Canada a cabinet that looks like Canada," he said after being sworn in. When asked by reporters to explain his decision for gender parity, his response was brief. "Because it's 2015," he said. Trudeau received worldwide attention for the move and called on world leaders to follow in his footsteps. He made the comment opposite when he was on a panel about gender equality and equal pay at the UN headquarters. However, at the start of his premiership, he was accused of not living up to his feminist rhetoric by failing to address the gender pay gap and counter violence against women. Some critics even branded him a "fake feminist."

Despite the criticism of Trudeau, the gender balance of his government was still unusual compared with others around the world. In 2017, the UN Women and the Inter-Parliamentary Union reported that the number of women in parliaments worldwide had stagnated, with 22.8 percent of national parliamentary positions taken by women (up from 11.3 percent in 1995) and only 18.3 percent of ministerial positions. Only five other countries had surpassed the 50:50 gender split in cabinet that Trudeau had committed to: Slovenia, Sweden, Nicaragua, France, and Bulgaria. The UK lagged behind considerably with 30.8 percent, and the USA fared even worse. Since FDR appointed Frances Perkins to his cabinet in 1933 (see page 131), only 52 women have made the cut. According to the Rutgers Center for American Women and Politics, the start of Donald Trump's presidency saw only 22 percent of senior cabinet positions held by women.

Yeah, I'm a nasty woman—
a loud, vulgar, proud woman.

100

ASHLEY JUDD
b. 1968

SOURCE: "Nasty Woman" by Nina Donovan
DATE: 2017
FIELD: Activism

On January 21, 2017, it was estimated that nearly seven million people around the world took to the streets in solidarity with the Women's March on Washington. Organized to coincide with the first day of President Donald Trump's administration, in Washington, DC, alone an estimated 680,000 women, men, and children came together in the largest coordinated protest in American history, dwarfing the previous day's audience for the inauguration. The women-led movement sought to "harness the political power of diverse women and their communities to create transformative social change." The movement's "unity principles" stood for an end to violence against women, and for reproductive rights, workers' rights, disability rights, and environmental justice, among others. A year later, the Women's March launched a new initiative "Power to the Polls," a voter registration tour to galvanize voters and engage communities around the country.

At the Women's March, celebrated feminists—among them Gloria Steinem—politicians, human rights advocates, religious leaders, and famous entertainers took to the podium to deliver rallying cries, calls for change, and criticism of the new president. Activist and actress Ashley Judd chose to recite a work by Nina Donovan, a 19-year-old poet from Tennessee. Donovan's poem had been written in response to Trump's televised comment about presidential nominee Hillary Clinton, in which he referred to her as a "nasty woman" during a presidential debate. "I'm nasty like the battles my grandmothers fought to get me into that voting booth," Judd cried to a captivated crowd. "I'm nasty like Susan, Elizabeth, Eleanor, Amelia, Rosa, Gloria, Condoleezza, Sonia, Malala, Michelle, Hillary."

INDEX

CREDITS